Author photo

Other books
by Roger Bowen

Anthology of Children's Poetry (Ed)
Lunacy to Croquet
The Curate and the General
We think you ought ot go
Swansea Exile
Croquet at Budleigh Salterton
General Goodwyn
Memoirs

i

Roger Bowen was born in Swansea and lived and worked in London and East Devon for most of his life. He worked in industry in Exeter before retiring to Budleigh Salterton. During his career he was successively a member of the Engineering Industry Training Board, Chairman of the Chamber of Commerce in Exeter, Chairman of the EEF in the Southwest, a Governor of three schools, a member of the Employment Tribunals and for eight years he was the founder and organiser of the Budleigh Salterton Music Festival.

Doctor John Howard Norton
1815 - 1874

Victorian Physician

Roger Bowen

CONTENTS

Norton Timeline		vi and viii
Preface		1
Chapter one	Charles Norton moves to Wales	7
Chapter two	Education and training	17
Chapter three	John Howard Norton apprentice	23
Chapter four	John Howard Norton first job	27
Chapter five	Amroth Castle opens as an asylum	37
Chapter six	The Nortons' commercial interests	55
Chapter seven	Coal Mine development	63
Chapter eight	The Norton Family trust	69
Chapter nine	Mining in difficult times	77
Chapter ten	John Howard Norton dies	81
Chapter eleven	Extended Family Norton	85
References		89

ILLUSTRATIONS

Doctor John Howard Norton	iv
Greenhill House	xiv
Bedlam 1810	2
The Meadows	5
Passengers	13
Carmarthen	14
Maniac in a straight jacket 1838	15
Old lithograph of Amroth Castle circa17th C	18
Colliery meeting	40
Elizabeth Norton & Juliana Norton	47
Family Group and Dorothea	48
Beatrice Muriel and Dorothea Norton	49
Gertrude Norton	50
Henry Norton	51
Norton Family Crest	52
Liz and Charles on honeymoon	53
The gentleman colliery manager	54
Cross Hands colliery	61
Children working in a coal mine - against regulations	64
Pit pony at work in mine	66
Henry Norton	72
Old Brewery	73
Charles Henry Norton, son of Charles Barron Norton	74
Henry Norton	76

Norton timeline
(starting with John Howard Norton)

John Howard Norton apprenticed to a
Sheffield apothecary   1836

John Howard attends Ecole de Medicin Pari   1837

John Howard marries at age in 22 in Paris   1840

John Howard attends Edinburgh University
and receives the degree of MD   1840

Charles Barron (John Howard's father), moves to Carmarthen to
open a brewery   1841

John Howard is highly commended for his MD
thesis on Organic Chemistry in its connections
with animal physiology   1842

John Howard appointed Medical Superintendent,
Palermo   1842 to 1844

John Howard receives the MRCS degree in London
                                   1844

John Howard appointed GP in Southampton
                                   1844 - 1851

John Howard leases Amroth Castle   1851

John Howard applies to magistrates for a Lunatic Asylum licence	1851
John Howard closes asylum	1856
John Howard gives up lease of Amroth Castle and moves to Nantglas House	1857
Charles Barron Norton dies in at the house of his son William in Merthyr	1860
John Howard with brothers reopens Crosshands colliery Llanon	1869
John Howard Norton dies at Nantglas House, Cross Hands, Llanon	1884

Charles Barron Norton
(Dr John Howard Norton's father)

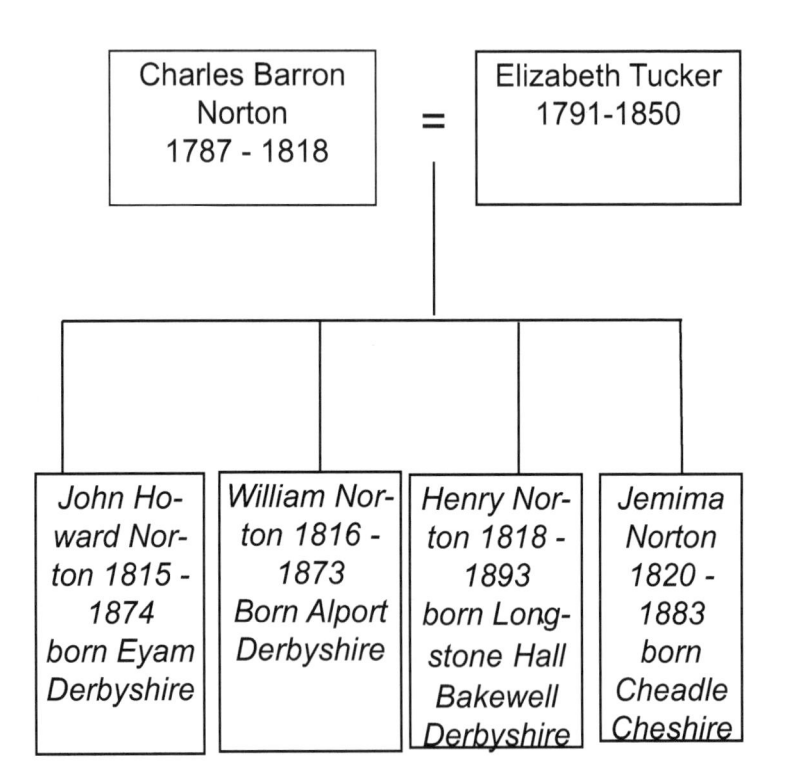

```
    Charles Barron              Elizabeth Tucker
        Norton           =          1791-1850
      1787 - 1818
```

| John Howard Norton 1815 - 1874 born Eyam Derbyshire | William Norton 1816 - 1873 Born Alport Derbyshire | Henry Norton 1818 - 1893 born Longstone Hall Bakewell Derbyshire | Jemima Norton 1820 - 1883 born Cheadle Cheshire |

Dr John Howard Norton

| Dr John Howard Norton 1815 - 1874 | = | Esther Thomas 1820 - 1871 |

| Elizabeth Norton 1842-1885 born Mwldan Cardiganshire | Mary Norton 1846-1890 born Stoneham Shirley Southampton | Esther Norton 1849 - 1849 born South Stoneham | Anne Robinson Norton 1853 - 1853 born Amroth Castle |

| Charles Henry Norton 1845 - 1899 born Millbrook Southampton | Howard John Norton 1848 - 1904 born Southampton | Juliana Norton 1851 - 1921 born Amroth Castle | William Talbot Norton 1858 - 1927 born Amroth Castle |

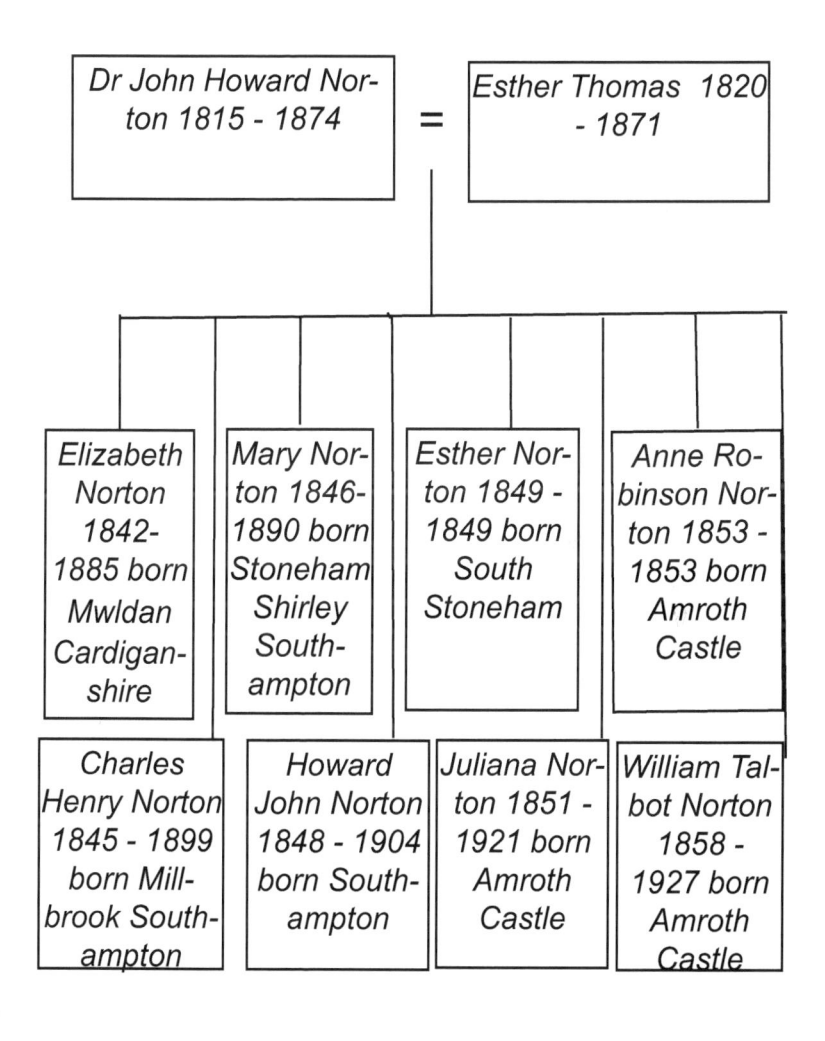

Victorian Physician

Greenhill House - the home of Charles Barron Norton

Roger Bowen

PREFACE

*Tomorrow, and tomorrow, and tomorrow,
Creeps in this petty pace from day to day,
To the last syllable of recorded time;
And all our yesterdays have lighted fools
The way to dusty death. Out, out, brief candle!*
                    Shakespeare 'Macbeth'

John Howard Norton started his education as a doctor after completing an apprenticeship with a Sheffield apothecary. Some of the problems he faced should be understood against the difficulties and privations that affected most of the population. Public Health in Victorian times was of very great concern and strenous efforts were directed at improvements.
In 1833 a severe outbreak of cholera affected many British towns and cities and prompted investigation on the part of the medical community. In 1842 Edwin Chadwick published his Report into the *Sanitary Conditions of the Labouring Population of Great Britain*. Edwin Chadwick was commissioned by the government to undertake an investigation into sanitation and make recommendations on

Victorian Physician

improving conditions. What followed was an independent and self-funded report . Chadwick found that there was a link between poor living standards and the spread and growth of disease. He recommended that the government should intervene by providing clean water, improving

The Bethlehem Asylum.
Known widely as "Bedlam" 1810

drainage systems and enabling local councils to clear away refuse from homes and streets. To persuade the government to act, Chadwick argued that the poor conditions endured by impoverished and ailing labourers were preventing them from working efficiently.

In 1848 the Public Health Act was passed by Robert Peel's government, establishing a *Central Board of Health* as well as corporate boroughs with responsibility for drainage and water supply to different areas. In 1849 Britain suffered another outbreak of cholera when 10,000 people died within three months in London alone.

In 1858 a revised *Public Health Act* was passed, abolishing the *Central Board of Health* and creating local boards responsible for preventative action and reform. Then in 1866 parliament passed the *Sanitary Act* making local authorities responsible for the removal of 'nuisances' to public health and for the removal or improvement of slum dwellings.

During the nineteenth century there was a huge growth in the population of Great Britain though the reason for this is not clear. There were large families, more children survived infancy and people were living longer. Imigration from Ireland during the potato famine and unemployment were reasons for this. By the end of the century there were three times more people living in Great Britain. There was also the industrial revolution when people flocked into towns in search of employment.

Large numbers of both skilled and unskilled people were looking for work, so wages were low, barely above subsistence level. Work was seasonal and men had not enough to live on when they were in work and had no savings to fall back on.

Children often worked long hours in dangerous jobs and in difficult situations for a very little wage. There were the climbing boys employed by the chimney sweeps and the little children who could scramble under machinery to retrieve cotton bobbins. Boys and girls worked in the coal mines, crawling through tunnels too narrow and low to take an adult. Children worked as errand boys, sweepers, shoe blacks, and sold matches, flowers and other cheap goods.

Low wages and the scramble for jobs meant that people needed to live near to where work was available. Time taken walking to and

Victorian Physician

from work could extend an already long day beyond endurance. Consequently available housing became scarce and expensive, resulting in overcrowded living conditions.

In his book *The Victorian Underworld*, Kellow Chesney gives a graphic description of the conditions in which many were living

'Hideous slums, some of them acres wide, some no more than crannies of obscure misery, make up a substantial part of the, metropolis ... In big, once handsome houses, thirty or more people of all ages may inhabit a single room,'

Many people could not afford the cost so they rented out space in their room to one or two lodgers who paid between twopence and fourpence a day.

Great wealth and extreme poverty lived side by side because the slums were side-by-side with the large houses of the rich.

This is the report he gave:

'As we gazed in horror at it, we saw drains and sewers emptying their filthy contents into it; we saw a whole tier of doorless privies in the open road, common to men and women built over it; we heard bucket after bucket of filth splash into it'.

Many cases of death caused by starvation and destitution were reported. In 1850 an inquest was held on a 38 year old man whose body was reported as being little more than a skeleton, his wife was described as being 'the very personification of want' and her child as a 'skeleton infant'.

There were children living with their families in these desperate situations but there were also numerous, homeless, destitute children living on the streets of London.

Many children were turned out of home and left to fend for themselves at an early age and many more ran away because of ill treatment.

In her book *The Victorian Town Child*, Pamela Horn writes:

Roger Bowen

The Meadows, Cross Hands the home of Dr John Howard Norton

'In 1848 Lord Ashley referred to more than thirty thousand 'naked, filthy, roaming lawless and deserted children, in and around the metropolis'

Many destitute children lived by stealing, and to the respectable Victorians they must have seemed a very real threat to society. Something had to be done about them to preserve law and order.
Many people thought that education was the answer and Ragged schools were started to meet the need. However there were dissenting voices against this. Henry Mayhew argued that

Victorian Physician

'since crime was not caused by illiteracy, it could not be cured by education ... the only certain effects being the emergence of a more skilful and sophisticated race of criminals'

One of the difficulties in dealing with the living conditions was the contemporary attitude:

'the poor were improvident, they wasted any money they had on drink and gambling';

As far as the later comment is concerned, this is clearly demonstrated in a hymn published in 1848 by Cecil Frances Alexander:

> *The rich man in his castle,*
> *The poor man at his gate,*
> *God made them, high and lowly,*
> *And order'd their estate.*

As the century progressed the plight of the poor, and of the destitute homeless children, impinged on the consciences of more and more people.
John Howard Norton had these challenges to face as he started his apprenticeship probably at age 12 in 1827. In Eyam the dreadful public health crisis was not as defined as it was in cities but in Sheffield it probably was. His lack of schooling told against him in starting in the medical profession but his apprenticship no doubt revealed the awful conditions that afficted the poor.

Roger Bowen

1

CHARLES BARRON NORTON MOVES TO WALES

> The baby in the cradle is crying,
> And the cat has scratched little Johnny.
> A little saucepan is boiling on the fire,
> A big saucepan is boiling on the floor...
> Traditional - lyrics of Sosban Fach

In moving from Derbyshire to Carmarthen, the county town of Carmarthenshire in Wales, Charles Norton, described as Gentleman, resident in Eyam was taking a risk
Carmarthen lies on the River Towy 8 miles (13 km) north of its estuary in Carmarthen Bay. Carmarthen has a claim to be the oldest town in Wales – Old Carmarthen and New Carmarthen became one borough in 1546. Carmarthen was the most populous borough in Wales in the 16th–18th centuries, described by William Camden as 'the chief citie of the country'. Growth was stagnating by the mid-19th century, as new economic centres developed in the South

Victorian Physician

Wales coalfield. In 1750, Wales was still an overwhelmingly rural country. Its population of about 500,000 was, however, gaining an expanding industrial base.
In the early 18th century, the industries established during the reign of Elizabeth I experienced a new vigour. Iron-making in Pontypool and Bersham, lead and silver mining in Flintshire and Cardiganshire, copper smelting in Neath and Swansea and coalmining in West Glamorgan and Flintshire increased substantially.
Nevertheless, they remained marginal in comparison with the agricultural economy. That economy was also developing, with the adoption of crop rotation, the use of lime, the enclosure of waste land and the development of proto-industrial production, especially in the woollen industry. When Britannia was a Roman province, Carmarthen was the civitas capital of the Demetae tribe, known as Moridunum ("Sea Fort"). It is possibly the oldest town in Wales, recorded by Ptolemy and in the Antonine Itinerary. The Roman fort is believed to date from about AD 75. A Roman coin hoard was found nearby in 2006. Near the fort is one of seven surviving Roman amphitheatres in Britain and only two in Roman Wales (the other being at Isca Augusta, Roman Caerleon). It was excavated in 1968. The arena itself is 50 by 30 yards (about 46 by 27 metres); the cavea (seating area) is 100 by 73 yards (92 by 67 metres). Veprauskas has argued for its identification as the Cair Guorthigirn ("Fort Vortigern") listed by Nennius among the 28 cities of Britain in his History of the Britains. Evidence of the early Roman town has been investigated for a number of years, uncovering urban sites likely to date from the second century
During the Middle Ages, the settlement was known as Llanteulyddog and accounted one of the seven principal sees (Cantrefi) in Dyfed. The strategic importance of Carmarthen was such that the Norman William fitz Baldwin built a castle there, probably about 1094. The current castle site is known to have been used since 1105. The castle itself was destroyed by Llywelyn the Great in 1215 but rebuilt in 1223, when permission was granted to build a town wall and crenellate the town, making it one of the first medieval walled towns in Wales. In 1405, the town was captured and the castle was sacked

Roger Bowen

by Owain Glyndŵr. The Black Book of Carmarthen, written about 1250, is associated with the town's Priory of SS John the Evangelist and Teulyddog.

The Black Death of 1347–49 arrived in Carmarthen through the thriving river trade. It destroyed and devastated villages such as Llanllwch. Local historians site the plague pit for the mass burial of the dead in the graveyard that adjoins the Maes-yr-Ysgol and Llys Model housing at the rear of St Catherine Street.

By 1851, Wales was the world's second leading industrial nation, behind England.

The take-off into self-sustained growth occurred in the second half of the 18th century. Yet development should not be predated. The counties of Wales were divided into hundreds; there were 88 in all and, as late as 1811, 79 of them had a majority of inhabitants still directly dependent upon the soil for their livelihood.

By 1851, however, two thirds of the families of Wales were supported by activities other than agriculture, which meant that, after the English, the Welsh were the world's second industrial nation.

The growth in heavy industry was fuelled by the wars - the Seven Years' War (1756-63), the American War of Independence (1775-83) and the French Revolutionary and Napoleonic Wars (1793-1802, 1803-15).

It was north-east Wales which developed the greatest range of industries. By the late 18th century there were 19 metalworks at Holywell and 14 potteries at Buckley; Holywell and Mold had cotton mills; lead and coal mines proliferated. Bersham, where the Wilkinson family were pioneers in the use of coke rather than charcoal in the smelting of iron, was one of Europe's leading ironworks.

By 1830 Monmouthshire and east Glamorgan were producing half the iron exported by Britain.

In the long term, however, the developments in the south east were more important. The ironworks of Merthyr Tydfil - Cyfarthfa and Dowlais in particular - gave rise to Wales's first industrial town. By 1830 Monmouthshire and east Glamorgan were producing half the iron exported by Britain.

Victorian Physician

Economic development was also significant in the Llanelli-Swansea-Neath area, in Amlwch with its vast copper mine, in Snowdonia where slate quarrying overtook copper mining, and in parts of central Wales where factory methods were replacing domestic production in the woollen industry.

Industry in Wales was concerned with the creation of capital rather than consumer goods. The iron-making centres produced iron rather than things made of iron; the metallurgical crafts which were so important to the prosperity of Sheffield and Birmingham struck few roots in Wales.

Methods were innovative: Cort's puddling process, invented in 1784, vastly sped up the rate of iron production and was so widely adopted in Wales that it become known as the Welsh method. In copper making, the Welsh process was acclaimed as one of the finest examples of skilled metallurgical art.

Industry in Wales was concerned with the creation of capital rather than consumer goods.

The factory system of the cotton industry was often considered to be the central feature of the industrial revolution, but the development of a new form of energy through the steam engine was perhaps the more significant. In this development Wales had a central role. Bersham produced most of the cylinders used in Watt's engines; the ironworks of Merthyr Tydfil rapidly adopted the new invention; the first experiment in locomotion was made in Wales and the country contributed enormously to the supply of fuel for steam engines.

Because of its reliance on coal, steam power had an impact upon the location of industry. In the late 18th century there was a degree of industrial liveliness to be found in almost all parts of Wales. By the mid 19th century it had become apparent that it was more economical to concentrate industrial activity in coalfields where engines could readily be supplied with fuel. Thus, while industries grew prodigiously in some regions of Wales, other areas experienced an industrial revolution which ultimately failed.

The early railway age provided a huge boost to the Welsh economy, both rural and industrial.

Roger Bowen

Many of Wales' industrial growth regions were difficult to access. The most favoured area was the north east. Served by the ports of the Dee estuary, and close to vibrant Lancashire, it was the first region of Wales to be integrated into the general system of turnpike roads.

The mountainous coalfield of the south presented greater problems. Initially Merthyr Tydfil was linked to Cardiff by packhorses carrying pig iron in paniers. A connecting road was built in 1767 but the great innovation was the waterway.

By 1800, all the main valleys of the southern coalfield were linked to ports via canals. The ports proved inadequate. The Marquess of Bute's initiative in securing a large masonry dock at Cardiff in 1839 was crucial to the subsequent development of the town. In 1841 the dock was linked to Merthyr by the Taff Vale Railway, making it possible for Cardiff to be a major exporter of coal as well as iron. The early railway age provided a huge boost to the Welsh economy, both rural and industrial.

The southern coalfield was the only upland coalfield in Britain. Elsewhere in Wales - in the hills of Flintshire and the mountains of Snowdonia - industry also developed in high altitude areas which had previously been thinly populated. Welsh industrial communities rarely had ancient civic roots, and the shape of the settlements was determined by the contours of the surrounding mountains. They were very much frontier societies, reliant for their growth on immigration.

At least until the later 19th century, the bulk of the immigrants came from rural Wales, giving rise to a largely Welsh-speaking urban proletariat. A high proportion of the immigrants consisted of footloose young men. This was one of the factors which caused early Welsh industrial communities to be of a highly inflammatory nature. The southern coalfield was disturbed by the *Scotch Cattle* unrest of the 1820s, the Merthyr Rising of 1831 and the Chartist upheavals of 1839. Such communities presented life threatening risks, with the lethal danger of the mines and furnaces, and the epidemics which threatened the lives of infants.

Nevertheless, such were the deprivations of rural life that the indus-

Victorian Physician

trial areas attracted a constant stream of migrants from the countryside. Between 1801 and 1841, Monmouthshire ranked first in the list of the most rapidly growing of the counties of Britain, and Glamorgan ranking third.

Charles Barron Norton, a long term resident in Derbyshire decided to move his business to Carmarthen where the Caramarthen United Breweries was founded in John Street.

At least as early as the 6th century, the Druidic legendary person Ceridwen is associated with cauldrons and intoxicating preparations of grain in herbs in many poems of Taliesin, particularly the Hanes Taliesin. This preparation, Gwîn a Bragawd, is said to have brought 'science, inspiration and immortality'.

The Welsh Triads attribute the introduction of brewing grains barley and wheat to Coll, and names Llonion in Pembrokeshire as the source of the best barley, while Maes Gwenith in Gwent produces superior wheat and bees.

The Anglo-Saxon Chronicle for 852 records a distinction between 'fine ale' and Welsh ale, also called bragawd. Bragawd, or braggot, is somewhat between mead and what we today think of as ale. Saxon-period Welsh ale was a heady, strong beverage, made with spices such as cinnamon, ginger and clove as well as herbs and honey. Bragawd was often prepared in monasteries, with *Tintern Abbey* and the *Friary of Carmarthen* producing the beverage until Henry VIII dissolved the monasteries in 1536.

In the *Laws of Hywel Dd*a, meanwhile, a distinction is drawn between bragawd and cwrwf, with bragawd being worth twice as much. Bragawd in this context is a fermented drink based on cwrwf to which honey, sweet wort, and ginger have been added.

Welsh beer is noted as a distinct style as late as 1854, with a recipe made solely from pale malt and hops described in a recipe book of the time.

In the mid-18th century, the Morgan family founded a small-scale ironworks at the east end of the town. In 1786 lead smelting was established to process the ore carried from Lord Cawdor's mines at Nantyrmwyn, in the north-east of Carmarthenshire. Neither of these firms survived for long. The lead smelting moved to Llanelli in 1811.

Roger Bowen

Passengers wait to be served on board

The ironworks evolved into tinplate works that had failed by about 1900. The borough corporation was reformed by a 1764 charter and again by the Municipal Corporations Act 1835.
In the late 18th century John Spurrell, an auctioneer from Bath, settled in Carmarthen. He was the grandson of Robert Spurrell, a Bath schoolmaster, who printed the first book, *The Elements of Chronology*, in the city in 1730. In 1840, a printing press was set up in Carmarthen by William Spurrell (1813–1889), who wrote a history

Victorian Physician

of the town and compiled and published a Welsh-English dictionary (first published 1848) and an English–Welsh dictionary (first published 1850). Today's Collins Welsh dictionary is known as the "Collins Spurrell". A local housing authority in Carmarthen is named Heol Spurrell in honour of the family.

The origins of Chartism in Wales can be traced to the foundation in the autumn of 1836 of Carmarthen Working Men's Association.

Carmarthen gaol, designed by John Nash, was in use from about 1789 until its demolition in 1922. The site is now occupied by County Hall, designed by Sir Percy Thomas. The gaol's "Felons' Register" of 1843–71 contains some of the earliest photographs of criminals in Britain. In 1843 the workhouse in Carmarthen was attacked by the Rebecca Rioters.

The revival of the Eisteddfod as an institution took place in Carmarthen in 1819. The town hosted the National Eisteddfod in 1867, 1911 and 1974, although at least in 1974, the Maes was at Abergwili.

Carmarthen Grammar School was founded in 1587 on a site now occupied by the old hospital in Priory Street. The school moved in the 1840s to Priory Row, before relocating to Richmond Terrace. At the turn of the 20th century, a local travelling circus buried one of its elephants that fell sick and died. The grave is under what was the

Carmarthen in 1850

Roger Bowen

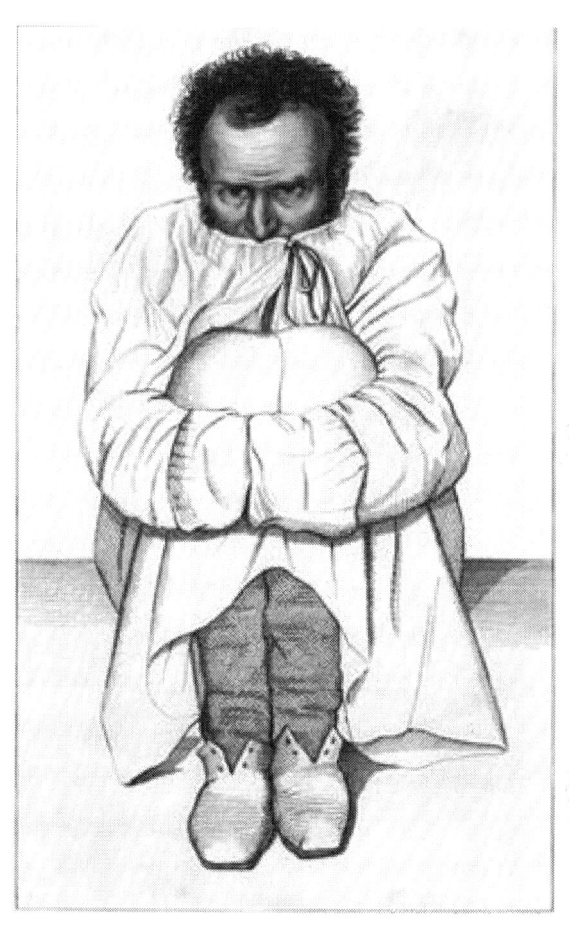

Maniac in a straight jacket 1838

rugby pitch.
During World War II, prisoner-of-war camps were situated in Johnstown (where the Davies Estate now stands) and at Glangwilli — the POW huts being used as part of the hospital since its inception. To the west of the town was the "*Carmarthen Stop Line*", one of a

Victorian Physician

Old lithograph of Amroth Castle circa17th C

network of defensive lines created in 1940–41 in case of invasion, with a series of ditches and pillboxes running north-south. Most of these structures have since been removed or filled in, but there are still two remains.
The Carmarthen community is bordered by those of Bronwydd, Abergwili, Llangunnor, Llandyfaelog, Llangain, Llangynog and Newchurch and Merthyr, all being in Carmarthenshire.
Carmarthen was named one of the best places to live in Wales.

Roger Bowen

2

JOHN HOWARD NORTON - EDUCATION AND TRAINING

There is a ship and she sails the sea
She's loaded deep, as deep can be
But not as deep as the love I'm i
I know not if I sink or swim
                    Scottish traditional

The first of the Nortons to emerge from the researches (undertaken by Julie Jones) is Henry Norton who lived from 1766 to 1828. The archive goes back much further in time than this but for the life of John Howard Norton this is adequate for our purpose.
The Norton family in the era starts with Charles Henry Barron Norton (1787 - 1860) who became an army surgeon starting from 1808 to 1812 as Ensign Norton and then was promoted Lieutenant and transferred to the 5th Garrison Battalion the 47th of Foot and subsequently to the 90th Foot in 1808.
47th (The Lancashire) Regiment of Foot was active from 1741–1881 There were two battalions, one established as Garrison/HQ at Fulwood Barracks, Lancashire called variously the The Cauliflowers, the Lancashire Lads, or even Wolfe's Own. They were active in the 1745 Jacobite Rising, the Napoleonic Wars and the Crimean War.

Victorian Physician

Amroth Castle as restored for use as an Asylum

Under the Childers Reforms the regiment amalgamated with the 81st Regiment of Foot (Loyal Lincoln Volunteers) to form the Loyal Regiment (North Lancashire) in 1881.

Charles' army career began in Manchester and continued in Marlborough until he moved to Carmarthen in South Wales around 1841. There he established breweries in the town and in Merthyr Tydfil. He married Elizabeth Tucker in 1814.

At the start of this account of the Norton Family Charles Henry established his growing family in Shepherd's Flat in Eyam Hall in Derbyshire in 1815 and then in 1818 at Great Longstone, finally moving to Cheadle, Cheshire in 1820. The village of Eyam is famous for the actions of its vicar, William Mompesson, in quarantining the inhabitants during the devasting bubonic plague of 1665-1666.

Charles Barron Norton fathered a family of three sons and a daughter all of whom moved with him from Derbyshire to Car-

Roger Bowen

marthen around 1841. The main brewery site was in Springfield and a pub, the Norton Arms, was established in Penyrgroes.
Two of his sons were prominent citizens of Carmarthen. Henry Norton JP (1816 - 1893) was mayor of the town living then at Greenhill House (see picture) and the subject of this biography Dr John Howard Norton (1815 - 1874), who became a physician living eventually in Llannnon, Carmarthen. John Howard was born in Eyam, and Henry Norton in Longstone Hall, Bakewell, Derbyshire. He died in Brewery House Bethesda Street, Merthyr Tydfil at the age of 74.
Mayor Henry had a daughter, Elizabeth (1846 - 1917) who was married in 1867 to Charles Henry Norton (1845 - 1899), (see early photo) the son of Dr John Howard Norton. They were first cousins. This latter Charles Henry Norton was ruined when his collieries collapsed due to flooding about 1884 when he was made bankrupt. He was prosecuted for an offence whilst in bankrupcy and then, in April 1895, with a criminal offence of embezzling the funds of two trusts. He was sentenced to 5 years in Swansea Prison. After this he went to the workhouse and died at home in 1899. His wife, Elizabeth moved into Greenhill House in 1891 and then to London after 1901 and died in 1917.
The Nortons were heavy investors in coal mines as were many wealthy people in 1850 and after. Collieries changed hands regularly as the coal trade waxed and waned. Sometimes an investor was caught with a mine that either ran out of seam or was flooded. Then it was a case of shutting up shop quickly before costs got out of hand. To save a flooded mine was both expensive and risky because large pumps could be required and run continually whilst the mine was being worked. The minute a mine was closed the pumps were withdrawn and sold before anything else because they were so valuable. As a footnote there were so many small mines in the Carmarthen region that the chances of winning coal at the right cost were quite small if one needed to pump.
A few years ago Roger Bowen wrote a book *Lunacy to Croquet* which decribed the life and achievements of an extraordinary man - doctor, literary pioneer and widely published historian - who lived in Budleigh Salterton in Devon. This was Thomas Brushfield (1827 -

Victorian Physician

1910) who, for all his other works will be remembered as one of the first specialist psychiatrists in the country. Writing about Brushfield's career and work provided an interest in the mental health of the nation in the 17th and 18th centuries, long before the NHS made efforts to come to grips with the problems we now ascribe to many and various medical conditions. In the 17th century specialised treatment for the 'feeble minded', as they were known, was not simply rudimentary but absent entirely.

Thomas Brushfield became a doctor in 1840 first studying medicine at the London Hospital. He started his professional career at the *Bethlehem Hospital* (known as *Bedlam* by inmates and locals, see picture) who used its open doors policy as a place of entertainment and a source of income from visitors. It became good family fun to tour the wards to inspect the wretched half-clothed inmates as they cried and pulled at the chains that secured them to their iron bedsteads. Brushfield moved on to other hospitals as his progress in the study of mental disorders progressed.

Brushfield's career was almost entirely with the insane and, until his forced retirement as a result of an injury at work, retired to Budleigh Salterton, Devon in 1869, was spent latterly as a medical superindent of lunatic asylums.

John Howard Norton's medical career started when he was apprenticed to an apothecary in Sheffield at an early age - 12 years old was normal; an apprenticship commonly lasting 7 years. His motivation in choosing medicine as a career was no doubt fostered by his father, Charles Barron Norton, who made his living as an army surgeon.

In England, as early as the 12th century, apothecaries (pharmacist physicians) belonged to the *Worshipful Company of Grocers*. This guild included the *Pepperers and Spicers* and apothecary shops sold everything from confectionery, perfumes, spices, spiced wines, to herbs and drugs that were compounded and dispensed on the premises to the public. By the mid-16th century apothecaries were equivalent to today's compounding chemists, preparing and selling substances for medicinal purposes.

Lack of regulation of this early pharmaceutical industry and the ease

Roger Bowen

in which fraudulent apothecary-physicians known as 'quacks' could advertise and dispense 'remedies' meant that apothecaries were never given the respect they desired as learned medical men. Sir Samuel Garth's satirical look at the apothecary's shop in *The Dispensary* reflects this entrenched negative attitude toward apothecaries at the beginning of the 18th Century:

> *Here, Mummies lay most reverently stale*
> *And there, the Tortoise hung her Coat o' Mail*
> *Not far from some huge Shark's devouring head*
> *The flying Fish their finny Pinions spread.*
> *Aloft in Rows large Poppy Heads were strung,*
> *And here, a scaly Alligator hung.*
> *In this place, Drugs in musty Heaps decay'd,*
> *In that, dry'd Bladders, and drawn Teeth were laid.*

The landmark ruling of 1704 had given the apothecary legitimacy on paper, but it took a century - up until *The Apothecaries' Act* of 1815, which granted apothecaries, amongst other rights, license to practice and regulate medicine, to slowly change the perceptions of the class-conscious Englishman as to the role and position of the apothecary in society.

The *Worshipful Company of Apothecaries* made great strides in ensuring that the calling became professional by overseeing apprenticeships, by registering master apothecaries and holding examinations for apprentices once their tenure with a master was completed.

Boys - and they were all boys - as young as 12 were 'bound' by way of an apprenticeship indenture to a master for seven years - the usual term to serve an apprenticeship for any trade or profession. An apprenticeship indenture was a legally binding document and money was paid to the master by a parent or guardian in exchange for the master agreeing to train the boy in their profession, and to supply the apprentice with food, clothing and lodging for the duration of the seven-year apprenticeship.

During the apprenticeship a boy was taught to compound pharmaco-

Victorian Physician

poeia preparations, recognize drugs and their use and to dispense complicated prescriptions. Throughout the 18th Century, most medicines were derived from herbs, plants and vegetables and such as the *Chelsea Physic Garden* served as a place of instruction for the apothecary's apprentice, providing simples and raw materials for the drugs manufactured in the laboratory of the Apothecaries' Hall attached to the headquarters of the *Company of Worshipful Apothecaries*. An apprentice attended lectures and demonstrations in the hall of Barber-Surgeons and could participate in anatomical dissections if they wished. However, the *Company of Worshipful Apothecaries* did not require an apprentice to be examined on his expertise as a surgeon; it was left entirely up to the apprentice to practice and become expert if he wished to use his skills as a surgeon which is the reason why barber-surgeons frowned on apothecaries who 'crossed the line' and not only dispensed medicines and attended patients for general medical complaints but performed surgery—an extremely risky venture in the pre-anesthetic and unhygienic conditions of the 1800's.

Masters usually took on one apprentice but there were instances of masters binding seven apprentices to his service. Given that parents paid a premium for their sons to be educated as apothecaries, these boys were less open to abuse. However, mistreatment at the hands of masters happened, and there are cases of boys being beaten, starved, worked almost death and made to live in appalling conditions. The usual place these apprentices lived out their seven years was at the back of the apothecary shop, in the workroom or 'laboratory' with the herbs and powders, medicinals and apparatus needed for compounding. An unsafe place for a young boy if the master did not take the boy into his home and thus share his table and company of his friends and family.

Roger Bowen

3

JOHN HOWARD NORTON
APPRENTICE

*Oh, love is gentle, and love is kind
The sweetest flower when first it's new
But love grows old and waxes cold
And fades away like the mornin' dew*
         Scottish Traditional

John Howard Norton made good progress as an apprentice and was advised, most likely by his apothecary master, to think about extending his education by seeking admission to a medical school. This advice was no doubt very welcome both to John Howard and to his father. But it would not have been easy advice to follow.
In 1830 university education for the degree of MD was very limited and open only to those who had a sufficient record of fashionable schooling and sufficient wealth and social standing. The foremost universities offering the degree of MD were Oxford and Cambridge which institutions enjoyed, for many years, a monopoly in the profession though other universities were beginning to appear. Some idea of the difficulty facing young people seeking introduction to the older institutions is gained when it is realised that the university course at the older universities required a study at school of Greek and Latin to a competent level.
Whatever the difficulties John Howard Norton was advised to make

Victorian Physician

application to the newly opened *Ecole de Medecin* - a school within Paris University. He was accepted in 1837 at the age of 19. This French school building housing the medical faculty was first opened in 1794 and later became by decree the *Imperial University of France* on the 17 March 1808. It was therefore fairly new iin its origin when John Howard Norton applied and was accepted following his successful introduction to the study of medicine as an apprentice to a Sheffield apothecary.

Normally entrance to a medical school in Britain would have been difficult for someone of his education or lack of it so the new French school probably provided a more accessible entrance procedure.

There is some evidence that Paris University was becoming aware of the shortage of university places for medecine and so were making stenuous effort to rectify the situation. This is probably why John Howard was offered a place.

It was here that he learned to speak French and reached a remarkable standard in that language within just one year. John Howard was married in 1840 in the British Embassy in Paris to Esther Thomas who, though born iin LLandyfriog, Cardiganshire, evidently had reason to move to Paris.

John Howard did well in Paris and then received advice that to progress in the medical profession he would be wise to obtain the degree of MD. This required that he was accepted for a place at a British university. Accordingly in 1841 he applied to and was accepted by Edinburgh University to read for the degree of MD.

Although the University of Edinburgh's *Faculty of Medicine* was not formally organised until 1726, medicine had been taught at Edinburgh since the beginning of the sixteenth century. Its formation was dependent on the incorporation of the *Surgeons and Barber Surgeons*. The foundation of the *Royal College of Physicians of Edinburgh* took place in in 1681.

The University was modelled on the *University of Bologna*, but medical teaching was based on that of the sixteenth century *University of Padua,* and later on the *University of Leiden* (where most of the founding faculty had studied) in an attempt to attract foreign students, and maintain potential Scottish students in Scotland.

Roger Bowen

Since the Renaissance the primary facet of medical teaching here was anatomy and, therefore, Alexander Monro primus was appointed Professor of Anatomy in 1720. Later his son and grandson (both of the same name) held the position, establishing a reign of Professor Alexander Monros lasting 128 years. In subsequent years four further chairs completed the faculty allowing it to grant the qualification of *Doctor of Medicine* (MD) without the assistance of the *Royal College of Physicians*.
Success in the teaching of medicine and surgery through the eighteenth century was achieved thanks to the first teaching hospital, town physicians and the *Town Guild of Barber Surgeons* (later to become the Royal College of Surgeons of Edinburgh). By 1764 the number of medical students was so great that a new 200-seat Anatomy Theatre was built in the College Garden. Throughout the 18th century until the First World War the *Edinburgh Medical School* was widely considered the best medical school in the English speaking world. Students were attracted to the Edinburgh Medical School from Ireland, America and the Colonies by a succession of brilliant teachers, such as William Cullen, James Gregory and Joseph Black, the opportunities afforded by the Royal Medical Society and a flourishing Extra-Mural School. John Howard Norton was fortunate indeed to obtain a place at such a prestigious university!
In the 1860s the medical school was within the Old College and by 1880 the new Royal Infirmary had been built on Lauriston Place. The construction of new medical buildings began and they were completed by 1888, in Teviot Place, adjacent to the Royal Infirmary. Together they housed the Medical Faculty with proper facilities for teaching, scientific research and practical laboratories. This complex came to be known as the "New Quad," in contrast to the Old College (sometimes known as the "Old Quad") and New College, which was not originally part of the university.
John Howard became Dr John Howard Norton following the successful completion of his course of study and received the degree of MD in 1843.
He received his first appointment shortly after as medical superendent in Palermo, Sicily.

Victorian Physician

Roger Bowen

4

JOHN HOWARD NORTON'S FIRST APPOINTMENTS

The water is wide, I cannot get o'er
Neither have I the wings to fly
Give me a boat that can carry two
And both shall row my love and I
                Scottish Traditional

Why was John Howard appointed as medical supertinendant in Sicily in the early 1840s? The answer is given by the following description of poor health and the fear of cholera:

In 1837 in Sicily, a liberal movement for independence from the Bourbon king was spreading among educated nobles like the Bentivegna family of Corleone, guildsmen, dissident groups including the Carbonari and Freemasons, and criminals, the latter of whom learned of the political movement in prison. The revolutionary leaders of 1848 and 1860, Francesco Bentivegna and Giuseppe Garibaldi, were both Republicans. In the year of Bentivegna's revolt, 1848, there would be another outbreak of cholera, and again in 1867, but in 1837, when Francesco Bentivegna was seventeen

Victorian Physician

years old, a third of his town fell ill, and half of those people died. That was the year he became a believer in Republicanism.

"Colera," in Italian as well as in Spanish, has two meanings: the deadly disease caused by various strains of Vibrio cholerae, and emotional passion, which people once believed was caused by an excess of bile. In the novel, *Love in the Time of Cholera*, Gabriel García Márquez uses the word's double meaning to warn against the dangers of an excess of passion!

In the days when health was still a matter of balancing the bodily humors, cholera morbus was a catchall term for any kind of stomach flu. 'Morbus' sounds worse in English than its meaning in Latin, 'hich is simply 'disease' or 'ailment.' Cholera is derived from the Greek *khole* which means 'illness from bile.'

'Asiatic cholera', which is what we recognize today as the deadly disease, cholera, caused by various strains of vibrio cholerae, used to be thought of as merely a more aggravated form of cholera morbus. It is understandable that there was enormous fear of disease in Sicily in the 1840s and some improvement in the provision of professional assistance became very necessary.

So it was that Dr John Howard spent 2 years in Palermo in an effort to improve Sicilian health care. This was just before the revolution of 1848 which he missed more by luck than judgement!

From London on the way to Sicily Dr John Howard Norton obtained his MRCS.

He then returned to England and took up an appointment as a GP in Southampton, for the period 1844 - 1851. What experience had he to offer the medical appointsment board then? Almost certianly it was his experience of the cholera outbreak in Palermo that was decisive.

Cholera reached the UK in 1832 having travelled from Russia and across Europe. Known as 'King Cholera' it claimed over 50,000 lives. The authorities struggled to cope with the outbreak. Though they had some warning that a cholera outbreak was likely some chose to deny this, probably on economic grounds. They did not want any interruption to trade. Also, at this time, there was no tradi-

Roger Bowen

tion, or widely accepted view, that local authorities, such as they were, should interfere in matters of health or hygiene, or tax the local population to raise money in order to introduce services to deal with the epidemic. There was no national health service, nor was there a borough council. There were a number of smaller, more parochial, vestries and parishes, along with the Town Trustees. As the seriousness of the situation was felt a local Board of Health was established to try and coordinate a response.

During September 1854, many people died in the centre of London in a series of cholera outbreaks. Dr. John Snow, a academic scientist, thought that because drinking water was provided by different competing water companies operating public pumps around the city that these locations seemed to fit well as sources of infection. He resolved to research the source of the water. He found that very many of the water companies took their supplies directly from the River Thames.

London had suffered many previous outbreaks of disease before the 1853 outbreak, including in 1832 and the worst outbreak of all which killed many residents in 1849. Snow published his first paper outlining his theory of water-borne disease and then in 1854 he tested his theory.

He prepared a map detailing deaths and their locations on a map of the water district. He found that a particular water pump on Broad Street was at the centre of a wide outbreak of the disease he had identified as cholera morbus.. The Broad Street pump was very close to an open cesspool that was known to emit foul odours. Snow disabled the pump and though the disease outbreak was already declining he got the credit for this.

The Reverend Henry Whitehead, a local priest and member of the parish inquiry committee had initially been a critic of Snow, but soon came to support Snow. He said:

"I must not omit to mention that if the removal of the pump-handle had nothing to do with checking the outbreak which had already run its course, it had probably everything to do with preventing a new outbreak, for the father of the infant, who slept in the same kitchen,

Victorian Physician

was attacked with cholera on the very day (September 8th) on which the pump-handle was removed. There can be no doubt that his discharges found their way into the cesspool and thence to the well. But, thanks to Dr. Snow, the handle was then gone."

A replica pump was displayed on the corner of Broadwick and Poland Street between 1992 to 2015, but was removed due to renovation at that location. However, this was never the true location of the original pump: for some time, this was marked by a red granite curbstone on the north side of the John Snow pub, situated on the corner of Broadwick and Lexington Street. In the summer of 2018, further renovation work placed the replica pump in the correct historical position. Every year members of the John Snow Society hold "Pumphandle Lectures" on subjects of public health, accompanied by a ceremony of removing and then re-attaching the pump handle.
Geographer at the University of Southampton Robin Wilson says: "John Snow represented the deaths in each street using rectangular blocks – the more blocks, the more cholera deaths which occurred at that location. It was a simple, but breakthrough way of visualising geographical clusters of disease, and ultimately saved many lives."
Now Robin has brought Snow's map into the 21st century by painstakingly geo-referencing every cholera death and pump location and transferring this to modern day maps , while also providing the digital tools for others to create their own versions.
He comments: "I have taken John Snow's original data and digitised it, allowing it to be overlaid onto modern maps and analysed using modern methods."
Snow's study was a major event in the history of public health and geography.
In the 1850s, cholera was believed to be spread by 'bad air' and germs weren't understood. His discovery helped change this and is widely regarded as the founding event of the science of epidemiology.

A geographer at the *University of Southampton* Robin Wilson says: "John Snow represented the deaths in each street using rectangular

Roger Bowen

blocks – the more blocks, the more cholera deaths which occurred at that location. It was a simple, but breakthrough way of visualising geographical clusters of disease, and ultimately saved many lives."
Robin brought Snow's map into the 21st century by painstakingly geo-referencing every cholera death and pump location and transferring this to modern day maps, while also providing the digital tools for others to create their own versions.

He comments: "I have taken John Snow's original data and digitised it, allowing it to be overlaid onto modern maps and analysed using modern methods. This should also allow some interesting 'mashups' to be created by others who are interested in interpreting Snow's findings in a modern context."

Snow's study was a major event in the history of public health and geography.

In the 1850s, cholera was believed to be spread by 'bad air' and germs weren't understood. His discovery helped change this and is widely regarded as the founding event of the science of epidemiology.

Several of John Howard Norton's children were born in Southampton: Charles Henry in Millbrook in 1845, Mary in South Stoneham, Shirley in 1846 and Howard John in 1848. Esther Norton was also born in Southampton in 1849 but did not survive for very long.

During the Napoleonic wars Southampton prospered because of the soldiers passing through on their way abroad. They spent lots of money in the town.

Furthermore by the early 19th century the port was booming again. Timber was imported from the Baltic, grain from Ireland and Eastern England. Coal, slate, and building stone were brought from Scotland. Also, wine and fruit were imported into Southampton from Portugal and Spain.

On the other hand Southampton lost its position as a seaside resort to Brighton. By 1820 sea-bathing had largely ceased. However, the quays at Southampton were not sufficient for the number of ships visiting the port. In 1838-42 a dock was built.

Also in the early 19th century many new shipyards were built along the Itchen. In 1822 a paddle steamer began running between South-

Victorian Physician

ampton and the Isle of Wight. In 1823 paddle steamers began running from Southampton to France and the Channel Islands. By 1830 100,000 people were travelling from Southampton by steamship every year.Between 1807 and 1809 the novelist Jane Austen lived in Southampton.

In the early 19th century the Saltmarsh, east of Southampton was drained and the land was sold for building houses. At the same time, the 4 fields north of Southampton were purchased by the town council and turned into parks. In the 1840s growth spread to Northam. Then in the 1850s, it spread to Freemantle and Newtown. In the 1860s many new houses were built in Shirley, St Denys, and Portswood and by 1900 growth spread to Swaythling. After 1900 Bitterne Park Estate was built.

In 1840 the railway reached Southampton. Stagecoach building was a major industry in the early 19th century but with the coming of railways it slowly declined. From the 1840s there were horse drawn buses in Southampton and from 1879 horse drawn trams. The trams were electrified after 1900.

There were several other improvements in 19th century Southampton. Gas street lights were installed in 1820. Then in 1836, the first modern police force was founded. In 1838 the Royal South Hampshire hospital opened. In 1846 the first cemetery opened near the southern end of the Common. In 1889 the first public library in Southampton opened in St Marys Street.

In common with most towns in the early 19th century Southampton was dreadfully unsanitary. The improvement commissioners only paved and cleaned the main streets and the back streets were very dirty. Out of 230 streets in the 1840s 145 were without sewers. In one case 77 people shared one toilet. Not surprisingly in 1849, there was a cholera epidemic in Southampton, which killed 240 people.

Life in 19th century Southampton gradually improved. After 1850 the town council took over the duties of the improvement commissioners. From then on all streets were cleaned and sewers were enlarged and improved. Nevertheless, there was another epidemic of cholera in Southampton in 1865, which killed 151 people. At first poor people obtained their water from conduits, wells or pumps but

Roger Bowen

in 1888 a new waterworks opened at Otterbourne. By that time most people had piped water.
No doubt this was a time when medical services were improving rapidly and this was the case as Dr John Howard Norton served as a general practionier there.
His first born child Elizabeth, who lived from 1842 - 1865 was born in Cardiganshire and there then followed those born in Southampton: Charles Henry, 1845 - 1899, in the borough of Milbrook. Mary in 1846 born in Shirley and Howard John in 1848. Esther died soon after birth there.
After his time in Southampton Dr Norton decided to change his career and so took a lease on the ancient castle of Amroth in Pembrokeshire.
Evidently the reason for moving to the large building that was Amroth Castle was Dr John Howard's developing interest in mental disorder. There is evidence that he was interested in the conditions giving rise to a demand for better care for the 'feeble minded' as those with mental health problems were known. His thesis during his time at Edinburg indicated this.
Conditions for mentally deficient patients during the first part of the eighteenth century were grim indeed.
During the 19th century there were various attempts to improve the condition of those detained in asylums, and various Acts of Parliament passed by champions of the cause such as Lord Ashley, Earl of Shaftesbury. Despite this there was no distinction between those who were suffering from mental illness such as schizophrenia and those who were mentally disabled or had learning difficulties, until the *1886 Idiots Act* which enabled the building of 'idiot asylums' or 'mental deficiency colonies'.
Records dating back as far as 1670 show that private mental health facilities or 'madhouses' were in existence but it was not until a century later that there was any attempt to inspect and regulate them.
At this time mental health treatment had not been developed and so conditions which we recognise and treat today were considered signs of madness. Those displaying symptoms were locked away from society and very often left to die in squalid and inhumane con-

Victorian Physician

ditions. Over time society used these institutions as places to lock away those who they felt weren't 'like them', including those with what we now consider to be low-level learning difficulties. Melancholy, wilfulness and 'possession by evil spirits' could be reasons for committal to the madhouse. Husbands who could afford to pay a sympathetic doctor could have their wives imprisoned at the madhouse with no just cause other than they would not obey their spouse. Whilst inside an inmate had no legal redress and no means to fight for their release as they were refused contact with any visitors.

It wasn't until the 18th century that the science of psychiatry began to develop, and with it came changes in the way that society treated the mentally ill. The 18th century was a time of great reflection and 'enlightenment' and changes in science which saw the belief in evil spirits regarded as superstition. Doctors and scientists began to understand about the workings of the brain and the nervous system, and so began the slow progress of mental health treatment.

The 1774 Lunacy Act saw the beginning of regulation with medical certificates from two separate doctors being required before a person could be committed, madhouses had to be registered and annually inspected, and a register of all inmates had to be held by a central authority. The Act was a huge step forward although it did not stop sane people from being detained. Neither did it give Magistrates powers to release people, although having regular inspections made it easier for them to petition for release. Following an assassination attempt on George III in 1800, the *Criminal Lunacy Act* was passed followed eight years later by the *County Asylum Act* which saw the building of new institutions specifically for the criminally insane. This began a process that saw patients with mental health issues being assessed and sent to different institutions depending on the nature of their condition.

At the turn of the 19th century insanity came to the fore, with the monarch's illness widely reported, as George III suffered bouts of insanity from 1788 until his death in 1820. Shortly after this Alexander Morison, a physician and inspector of the Surrey madhouses, started lecturing on mental diseases, the first formal lectures on psy-

Roger Bowen

chiatry.

Despite this new found interest in the causes and treatment of mental illness it was not the *1833 Madhouse Amendment Act* that was responsible for the way patients were treated during the Victorian era, but the *1834 Poor Law*. This Act was responsible for the increase in the number of asylums and other similar institutions, as most of those who found themselves settled or permanent residents in the workhouses were those who could not fend for themselves: children, so more orphanages were built; the sick, so more hospitals were built; or those with mental illness or learning disabilities and so more asylums were built.

Throughout the latter part of the 19th century there were various attempts to improve the condition of those detained in asylums, and various Acts of Parliament passed by champions of the cause such as Lord Ashley, Earl of Shaftesbury. Despite this there was no distinction between those who were suffering from mental illness such as schizophrenia and those who were mentally disabled or had learning difficulties until the *1886 Idiots Act* which enabled the building of 'idiot asylums' or 'mental deficiency colonies'. These were the changes that helped Dr John Howard Norton to found an asylum in South Wales and assisted him in the new registration process.

Victorian Physician

Roger Bowen

5

AMROTH CASTLE OPENS AS AN ASYLUM

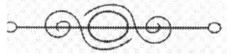

*O my Luve is like a red, red rose,
That's newly sprung in June:
O my Luve is like the melodie
That's sweetly play'd in tune.*
Robert Burns

The building now known as Amroth Castle was a feudal residence in the early medieval period which was noted by Fenton (in 1810) as being in the hands of John Elliott of Eareweare (the local name for the estate) in 1690 who paid tax on five hearths. It was acquired by the Elliott family in the 14th century. There was an earlier castle half a mile to the north of which little remains.
There was extensive rebuilding in the early 18th century but some earlier (probably 15th century) elements remain. Colonel Ackland acquired the property in 1790 and made a number of alterations and additions.
After passing through several hands, including the families of Biddulph and Bevan, the property was used by Dr John Howard Norton from 1851 to 1856 as a private lunatic asylum; it came into the

Victorian Physician

hands of the Fussell family in 1861 and was later owned and occupied by Owen Colby Philipps, the shipping magnate, who bought the White Star Line and was created Baron Kylsant of Carmarthen and Amroth in 1923.

The introduction and growth of county pauper lunatic asylums during the nineteenth century remains the subject of vigorous debate among social historians of medicine. The proportion of paupers classified as lunatics rose from one in a hundred in 1842 to one in eight by 1910.

Andrew Scull has suggested that the growth of commercialization, industrialization and of new conurbations led to the fragmentation of family relations and compelled more individuals to seek the institutional support of the New Poor Law.

Dr Norton made application to the magistrates for the establishment, in Amroth Castle, of a private lunatic asylum. The magistrates were doubtful. Though the *Poor Law Act* was helpful it was necessary to persuade local magistrates that the person making the application was competent, trustworthy and sincere. The premises had to be suitable for the accomodation of the mentally ill.

There then followed a lengthy debate as a result of whch the magistrates decided:

'*Amroth Castle would be allowed to accept 28 male and 28 female lunatics of whom not more than eight shall be private patients, for thirteen calendar months*'. Described earlier as '*a castellated mansion, delightfully situated on the coast, where the air is as mild and salubrious as in Devonshire*'.

In spite of having sent a second letter reinforcing their views, the Commissioners felt that it was likely that Norton's licence would be renewed by the court 'notwithstanding the manifest defects'.

A year later, on inspection, although the wards were 'less incommodious and comfortless', they saw no prospect that the major defects could ever be removed, as this would prove to be too expensive from the proprietor's point of view. The only redeeming feature concerning the site was that the grounds, unlike those at Haverfordwest, were sufficiently extensive to allow the patients 'healthful labour and recreation'.

Norton's detailed reply to a request for his views on various aspects of the management of the asylum might have misled an inexperienced observer, as it suggested that his treatment strategies compared favourably with those of the most forward-looking centres of the time.

The magistrates found that Dr Norton:

in an age when the training of most Pembrokeshire doctors was confined to apprenticeship, usually to a local surgeon, Dr Norton had received the best medical education available, and was sufficiently well qualified to have set himself up as a physician. His reasons for turning to psychiatry are not clear but it is likely that he went into the asylum-keeping business merely from profit-making motives.

John Howard's application to the Justices was successful, and he was allowed to accept '28 male and 28 female lunatics of whom not more than eight shall be private patients, for thirteen calendar months'. Described earlier as 'a castellated mansion, delightfully situated on the coast, where the air is as mild and salubrious as in Devonshire', the house was first visited by the Lunacy Commissioners in April 1852. They found two private and sixteen pauper patients there, twelve of whom had been taken from an asylum in Glamorgan. The pauper patients were housed in the stable, which had been whitewashed and boarded, but few other structural changes had been made. The single bedrooms had been made from the horses' stalls. The male dormitories, placed in the loft, had no means of heating and were accessible by steps which were difficult to climb. The day rooms were 'gloomy and imperfectly furnished' and the Commissioners wrote to Richard James, the clerk to the visiting justices, expressing their strong disagreement with the principle of adopting such buildings for the care of the sick, and regretting that a licence should have been granted for 'premises so evidently entirely unsuited to the purpose'. The magistrates, on the other hand, were not slow to reply that they considered the place 'to

Victorian Physician

The numbers of men, many of them imigrants, employed in winning coal grew from 45,000 in 1801 to 450,000 by 1900.

be in every respect suitable as regards situation, accommodation and treatment'. In spite of having sent a second letter reinforcing their views, the Commissioners felt that it was likely that Norton's licence would be renewed by the court 'notwithstanding the manifest defects'.

A year later, although the wards were 'less incommodious and comfortless', they saw no prospect that the major defects could ever be removed, as this would prove to be too expensive from the proprietor's point of view. The only redeeming feature concerning the site was that the grounds, unlike those at Haverfordwest, were sufficiently extensive to allow the patients 'healthful labour and recreation'. Dr Norton's detailed reply to a request for his views on various aspects of the management of the mentally ill might have misled an inexperienced observer, as it suggested that his treatment strategies compared favourably with those of the most forward-looking centres of the time.

'I think that it may be laid down as a rule that the. management of the insane.should be the same as nearly as possible as for the sane and I consider that seclusion .as a means of punishment, is not only of no value, but is positively hurtful. The same may be said of punishment of any kind. I never allow it to be adopted, except as a means of separation, as for instance where two patients quarrel and require [sic] to be kept asunder to allow their tempers to cool. Restraint is both unnecessary and hurtful..but is at certain times indispensable. Sometimes patients. are better invested with a garment which prohibits the use of the hands as. they will the sooner lie down and sleep overcome them, than if allowed to irritate themselves by tearing and knocking about all night. In short, with careful and kind conduct on the part of the attendants, not one case in 100 requires restraint in the daytime. In this house, both restraint and seclusion are the sure exception, and patients are treated. in the same manner as those with whom they are associated in the performance of the duties of the farm, garden and household.'

It soon became apparent that the policies put into practice at the asylum differed from those described by Norton. During one inspection it was found that a patient had been fastened to a fixed chair by a strap around her waist almost continuously for long periods and at times she had been placed in a strait waistcoat. Their complaints included comments about the diet: 'rice milk is a very insufficient substitute for herrings' and the 'very cheerless and gloomy dayrooms' met with no reponse from the magistrates. Nor did the justices pay any more attention to the legal rights of those accepted as patients at Amroth Castle. In order to minimise the risk of illegal detention, the law required that scrupulous attention should be paid to details concerning the compulsory admission of patients. The most

Victorian Physician

serious breach of legal protocol occurred when the certificate used to detain the patient 'was wholly insufficient' and, presumably, Norton had no alternative but to allow him to leave, regardless of his clinical state. Having considered these matters carefully, Shaftsbury acknowledged :

that magistrate's opinions: are not always in agreement with the views expressed by Visiting Commissioners as to the shortcomings [and] it is only in cases of great abuse that we can feel justified in adopting the extreme course of applying to your Lordship for a revocation of the license.

Having considered the evidence the Lord Chancellor agreed that Amroth Castle should be closed. Norton appealed against the decision, but it was decided that 'a more satisfactory and skilful management than that of Dr Norton was called for'. Ultimately, the visitors asked for help in providing 'efficient medical superintendence for the remaining term of Dr Norton's license' but were informed that this matter 'belongs peculiarly to the visiting justices'. The house was closed in 1856.

Norton relinquished his lease of Amroth Castle and assumed the role of a minor industrialist in the operation of coal mines in Carmarthenshire.

As a psychiatrist Norton presents as something of an enigma. Apart from having the best medical training available, he became a member of the Association which is now the *Royal College of Psychiatrists*. This was an organisation which generally attracted only the most progressive of asylum doctors. Yet, with his low professional standards and unwillingness to accept change, he must be judged a failure in the field of the care of the insane.

Negotiations between the *Quarter Sessions Courts* of the West Wales counties and that of Glamorgan had started in the 1840s in the hope that accommodation for pauper patients from the four counties could be made available on one site. Had that been brought about, the Haverfordwest asylum would certainly have been closed earlier and Amroth Castle might not have been opened. On the other

Roger Bowen

hand, had the scheme proceeded before the Glamorgan authorities left the partnership, the new building would have been in the Swansea district, which might have proved a hindrance in the development of a more locally-based service in Dyfed in a later age. At first it was uncertain whether Haverfordwest, with its special status as a 'town and county of the town', would be included. A document in the Francis Green papers shows that counsel's opinion was sought on the matter, and suggests that the magistrates may have had some reservations about proceeding with the union, particularly in view of their belief that 'there is at present a lunatic asylum at Haverfordwest sufficiently large for the accommodation of the lunatics belonging to the town'. However, a contract, separate from that of Pembrokeshire, was eventually made with the joint committee of magistrates and by 1858 Lord Cawdor reported that a site had been bought at Carmarthen and that of the total cost of the scheme, £41,940, Pembrokeshire must contribute £13,800 and Haverfordwest £840. Later under the provisions of one of the *Lunacy Acts*, it was decided that the town must be 'removed from its previous legal position as a county' so that it could be treated as part of the county of Pembroke.

Distant though it was from Pembrokeshire, the opening of the new asylum at Carmarthen in 1865 brought about the introduction of a new phase in the management of the mentally ill in west Wales. No longer would the primitive conditions that had caused so much concern for so long be tolerated. However, the availability of new resources did not guarantee that full use would be made of them. Fourteen years later, nearly 60% of the county's mentally-ill population were still being cared for by 'relatives and others', which only too often meant that their needs were totally ignored. During this century, the whole practice of psychiatry has been transformed, and with the development of increasingly effective ways of dealing with mental illness, it is now desirable that as many as possible of those who seek help from the mental health services should be treated in the community to which they belong. Although the need for inpatient psychiatric facilities is far less than ever before, for the forseeable future, a gradually decreasing number of patients are likely to need

Victorian Physician

Date	Colliery	Owner
1854-55		No listing
1856	Mynydd Newydd	Norton & Brothers
1857	Mynydd Mawr	Norton & Brothers
1858	Cross Hands, Mynydd Mawr	Norton & Sons
1859 - 68		do
1870	Cross Hands, California, Mynydd Mawr, Mynyddsil	Norton & Co
1871 - 74	Cross Hands, California	do
1875	Cross Hands, California, Victoria	do
1876	California, Cross Hands	do
1878 - 78	California, Cross Hands, Gilfach, Cawdor	do
1879	California, Old Cross, Gilfach	do
1880	Cross Hands, Gilfach	Norton & Co

Roger Bowen

at least part of their treatment in a hospital setting. It is perhaps fitting that, among the foremost of the changes introduced into the county in the course of this century, has been the opening of a psychiatric unit in the new general hospital situated, appropriately enough, at Haverfordwest.

Victorian Physician

Roger Bowen

Elizabeth Norton, daughter to Henry & Margaret Norton, born 1846

John Howard Norton's daughter Juliana in 1875

Victorian Physician

Family group with maid and nurse including Ethel, Juliana, Juliana, and Gertrude. Ethel and Eliza are in attendance.
Below: Dorathea daughter of Charles Henry Norton

Roger Bowen

Above: Beatrice Muriel in 1919. Below: Dorothea, granddaughter of Jemima Norton

Victorian Physician

Gertrude Thompson nee Norton in 1926

Roger Bowen

Charles Henry Norton born 1845

Victorian Physician

The Norton Family Crest as designed and drawn by Henry Norton, brother of Dr John Howard Norton

Roger Bowen

Elizabeth with Charles Norton on their honeymoon in 1867

Victorian Physician

The gentleman colliery manager

Roger Bowen

6

THE NORTON'S COMMERCIAL INTERESTS

*Till a' the seas gang dry, my Dear,
And the rocks melt wi' the sun:
And I will luve thee still, my Dear,
While the sands o' life shall run.*
                              Robert Burns

It was in 1841 that Charles Barron Norton (father of Dr John Howard Norton) became interested in the brewing industry and established two breweries and a pub in Carmarthen. His sons found the venture attractive and so joined him. This became a profitable concern and the partnership of father and three sons flourished for many years. Most will recognise the modern Buckley's Brewery Ltd but few may realise that this large brewary owes its formation, in part, to the Norton Brothers. The Norton Brothers and Carmarthen Brewary com-

Victorian Physician

bined to become Carmarthen United Brewaries. This happened after the death of Charles Norton when the Norton and Sons became the Norton Brothers.

The brewery between the bottom of Thomas Street and the River Lliedi owes its origins to Henry Childs, who, from 1769, developed a substantial malting, brewing and public house venture, basing himself at the Falcon, a public house which would later become the offices of Buckley's Brewery. In 1798, Childs's daughter married the Rev. James Buckley, who was later remembered in the name of one of Buckley's (and later Brains's) ales. When Childs died in 1824, Buckley took over the brewery but also died fifteen years later and was succeeded in the business by his son James, who would in turn pass the business on to his own sons, James and William in 1883. The business expanded greatly in the late nineteenth-century forming Buckley's Brewery Limited in December 1894, amalgamating Messrs W. Bythway and Co Brewery (NPRN 466) in 1896 and Carmarthen United Breweries Limited (itself an amalgamation of Norton Brothers and Carmarthen Brewery) shortly thereafter. In 1903, it was granted a *Royal Warrant of Appointment* as brewers to the Prince of Wales, and in 1910 when George V ascended to the throne, became brewers to the King. With this success the site expanded accordingly with the construction of new buildings on the site along the river.

Carmarthen United Breweries Ltd, John Street, Carmarthen, Dyfed was registered in 1890 to acquire Norton Brothers (founded by 1847), Springside; David Evan Lewis & Sons, Merlin Brewery and Evans & Son, all of Carmarthen. It was acquired by Buckley's Brewery Ltd. in 1900 when brewing in those names ceased.

Another attractive investment in the mind of Charles Barron was in local coal mines which were experiencing a huge and increasing demand for coal. He involved his sons (as Norton & Brothers and later as Norton and Sons) in 1856 which was very convenient for John Howard who was finding the business of funding the Amroth lunatic asylum difficult to the point of having to shut down the enterprise on the instructions of the auhorities. John Howard now urgently needed a new soure of income and so the success and enterprise of father

Roger Bowen

came as a welcome release.
Coal extraction was a growth industry for South Wales at this time. It was also a great magnet for investors who flooded into the market. 'Black gold' some called the coal found in the Rhondda and Cynon Valleys of South Wales during the mid-nineteenth century. The invention of coal-powered steam engines revolutionized the Welsh economy as world demand for coal skyrocketed. The landscape was changed drastically as the trees of green valleys were cut down to support the coal mines carved into the Welsh hills. By 1870, coal production in the area had surpassed 13 million tons. Local farming communities grew smaller as families swapped unstable agricultural lives for the steady wages of mining. But it was a dangerous trade: the mines averaged a death every 6 hours and a serious injury every 12 minutes! Still, immigrants from Ireland, Scotland, and the English Midlands flooded the valleys to dig in the narrow tunnels. The influx hastened the demise of the Welsh language and fuelled the birth of the nation's modern cities.
Cross Hands is a village in Carmarthenshire approximately 12 miles from Carmarthen. The continuous built up area which includes the villages of Cross Hands, Gorslas, Cefneithin and Pen-y-groes had a population of 5,717 in 2011.
The South Wales Coalfield extends across parts of Pembrokeshire, Carmarthenshire, Swansea, Neath Port Talbot, Bridgend, Rhondda Cynon Taf, Merthyr Tydfil, Caerphilly, Blaenau Gwent and Torfaen. It comprises a fully exposed synclinorium with a varying thickness of Coal Measures (Upper Carboniferous/ Pennsylvanian) deposits with thick, workable seams in the lower parts and generally thinner and sparser seams in the upper parts, together with a development of sandstones (Pennant Sandstone). These sandstones have been much used in building construction (including the characteristic terraces of former miners' houses) and this gave rise to bleak uplands rising 300–600 metres above sea level between the steep-sided valleys in which most deep mines were developed.
The coal generally increases in grade or 'rank' from east to west, with bituminous coals in the east, and anthracite in the west, mostly

Victorian Physician

to the north and west of Neath. The Rhondda Valley was particularly known for steam coals which fuelled steamships of the 19th and early 20th centuries.
Communications along the valley floors provided the main routes for exporting coal south to ports and docks such as Newport Docks, Cardiff Docks and Barry Docks. Early activity was mainly by levels or adits driven into coal seams from outcrops in the valley sides. Development of the coalfield proceeded very actively from about 1850, when deep mining became significant in the previously entirely rural Rhondda Valley. Tramway-fed canals such as the Swansea Canal and Glamorganshire Canal were supplemented, and then superseded, by the development of numerous competing railway branches which fed docks principally at Swansea, Cardiff, Newport, Llanelli and Barry. Later colliery shafts were sunk as deep as 800 yards in order to reach the thicker, better quality seams.
Iron ore was also extracted from the coal measures, principally from the north crop area (including Merthyr Tydfil and Blaenavon). The availability of coal and nearby limestone (as a flux) gave rise to a substantial local iron and steel industry which was perpetuated in the 20th century by the location of modern steelworks at Ebbw Vale, Newport and Cardiff and Port Talbot. These used imported iron ore.
Coal workings were over-expanded in the late nineteenth century and the Welsh coal owners had failed to invest in mechanisation. By 1900 the South Wales Coalfield had the lowest productivity, highest costs and smallest profits in Britain. In *The Citadel* and the 1939 novel *How Green Was My Valley* (later filmed in a wildly inaccurate colliery village) describe such hardship, as do the poems of Idris Davies the miner, teacher and poet of Rhymney.
Following the general collapse of the UK coal industry, most pits closed in modern times with factors such as exhaustion of reserves and geological complexity adding to their problems. The last deep mine, at Tower Colliery on the north crop, ceased mining in January 2008. However, a few small licensed mines continue to work seams, mostly from outcrop, on the hillsides. Although some areas of the coalfield are effectively worked out, considerable reserves remain. However, the geological difficulties, which resulted in the closure of

Roger Bowen

Nantgarw colliery, make the cost of significant further extraction high. The coalfield experienced a late-stage development when opencast mining was commenced on a large scale, mostly on the gently-dipping north crop. In addition, old tips were reclaimed for their small coal content, which could be burned in power stations such as nearby Aberthaw. Most of the old sites have been filled and landscaped, but new operations continue.

As the mines and other industries rapidly expanded throughout the coalfield, nearby towns also expanded to meet the demand for labour. In the first half of the nineteenth century, the development of ironworks saw the population of Merthyr Tydfil, in the northern part of the coalfield, increase from 7,700 in 1801 to 49,794 in 1861, making it the largest town in Wales. This was, of course the primary interest of Norton & Sons whose fortunes flourished as a direct result.

As Cardiff and other ports in South Wales grew to meet the demands for exporting iron, steel and coal in the later part of the nineteenth century, valleys that had previously been sparsely inhabited suddenly increased in population. The Rhondda valley grew from less than a thousand people in 1851 to more than 150,000 in 1911.Between 1881 and 1911, Glamorgan became the most industrialised part of Wales and saw inward migration of more than 330,000 people from elsewhere in Wales, neighbouring parts of England and further afield.

Coal mining in the South Wales Coalfield was a dangerous occupation with lifelong health implications.

Between 1849 and 1853, miners over the age of 25 in the Merthyr Tydfil district were found to have a life expectancy of around 20 years, lower than in other mining areas of England and Wales.

In a list of collieries in production from 1854 the Norton & Sons interests in mining coal were widespread and continued into 1888 when the business was reformed. Dr John Howard died in 1874, his father died in 1860 and so for some years it was the other sons of Charles Barron Norton who ran the business.

A significant change took place in 1868 when the premises of the Cross Hands colliery came up for sale, it having been closed for a

Victorian Physician

number of years previous to this and was leased by the Norton Brothers. Meanwhile the Nortons had been engaged at Mynydd Newyth and Mynyth Mawr since 1856.
Cross Hands was placed admirably for the extraction of premium grade steam coal and so it quickly became highly productive.
The cities of south Wales expanded with the increased levels of coal passing through the docks. Cardiff, Swansea and Newport experienced huge population growth through the 19th century due to the economic expansions enabled by the trade.
By 1840 the canal and rail network enabled 4.5m tons of coal to be produced. Of this, 2.25m went to the steel industry, one million to the domestic market and other industries and 750,000 tons for export.
Just 14 years later, 8.8m tons were produced, with 2.6m exported. The Rhondda Valley experienced the highest growth in production. By 1874, 16.5m tons were produced, with a quarter of that figure exported. The rise of the Welsh coal industry seemed unstoppable, with high quality coal available in massive quantities.
The mines were privately owned throughout the 19th century as indeed were the Norton & Co collieries. It was viewed as an area of industry with potentially huge rewards for the investors and speculators, who obtained licences to sink shafts or expand existing mines.
Owners such as the members of the Norton family became members of the gentry, and many more made huge sums of money. It had knock-on effects for related industries and areas.
The early coal owners were the copper works and ironmasters. It was after 1840 that the successful coal collieries came into existence. (It must be remembered that the coal owners did not own the coal, but the equipment and buildings used in mining. The land belonged to Landlords, such as Lord Aberdare, who became very rich from the royalties earned). Many individuals, such as Thomas Powell, David Davies, John Nixon, W T Lewis (later Lord Merthyr), were able to set up successful colliery companies as not much capital was needed to start. Some formed limited liability companies as a way of increasing capital. As many coal owners were directors of a

Roger Bowen

The new Cross Hands colliery

number of colliery firms the directors held most of the shares and they grew rich. By 1873, most of the major colliery companies in South Wales had been formed, and by 1914, the giant combines such as the Cambrian Combine, United National and T Beynon and Company, dominated and controlled 40% of output. By this time the Norton extended family was out of the industry.

Some of the coal owners were from humble backgrounds, such as David Davies of Llandinam, who was the son of a small farmer in Montgomeryshire. He was one of first railway builders in Wales, which enabled him to raise the money to become a coal owner. Many of the early owners were Welsh; they lived in the new mining communities, spoke Welsh, were non-conformist and liberal (like the

Victorian Physician

miners). Some, such as Lord Merthyr, were generous and gave money for schools, chapels, institutes, libraries and hospitals. Many owners were also JPs, Poor Law Guardians, Councillors and MPs, such as Lord Rhondda, who controlled the Cambrian Combine, who was MP for Merthyr Tydfil from 1888 to 1910. By the end of the 19th century however, most of the owners had become removed from the daily life of the mining communities, living on big estates near Cardiff and Swansea, such as David Davies who lived in Montgomeryshire. The South Wales Coalowners Association was formed in 1873, and although the owners did not agree on all issues, they were all opposed to increases in wages and in trying to get higher productivity from their workers. They were concerned as the amount of coal raised per person was lower than anywhere else in Britain. The animosity that grew between the owners and the workers can be seen by the attitudes to the Powell Duffryn Coal Company, owned by Tom Powell, known as 'Poverty and Death'.

Roger Bowen

7
COAL MINE DEVELOPMENT

And fare thee weel, my only Luve!
And fare thee weel a while!
And I will come again, my Luve,
Tho' it were ten thousand mile.
                            Robert Burns

The *Llanelly and Mynydd Mawr Railway* was authorised in 1875. It made use of part of the long defunct *Carmarthenshire Railway or Tramroad* of 1801. The older line began running trains in 1803, and was a plateway of about 4 feet gauge, with horse traction, for the purpose of bringing minerals from the Mynydd Mawr to the sea for onward shipment at Llanelly Docks. A contributing factor encouraging the development of new and smaller coal workings was the development of rail lines and shipping faacilities.
The Llanelly and Mynydd Mawr line opened in 1881, worked by the contractor, John Waddell, who had built the line and taken a majority of the shares. The fortunes of the company were closely bound with those of the mineral industries, which fluctuated considerably. The Company considered operating a public passenger service but never did so, although workmen's trains were operated for some years.
In the 1760s the area around Llanelly had considerable colliery activity, and there were five short canals from pits to the sea shore;

Victorian Physician

the heavy mineral was brought to shipping for onward transport, at a time when there were no usable roads or railways.

In 1769 Kymer's Canal was opened between pits in the Gwendraeth Valley and the coast; there were a number of basic wooden tramways in connection with it, covering the short distance between the mouth of the pits and the nearby canal.

At that time coal was loaded into ships at Llanelly by beaching them on the mudflats, or using lighters to ferry coal out to larger vessels anchored off-shore. Wharves were an obvious solution, and one of the first was built in 1795 to serve a canal from pits owned by William Roderick, Thomas Bowen and Margaret Griffiths. This was later developed as the Pemberton's Dock.

In March 1797 Alexander Raby arranged a lease with Dame Mary Mansell, owner of the Stradey Estate, entitling him to work coal measures on the estate. Raby undertook to mine 5,000 tons of coal annually and there were penalties if he failed to do so (or to pay the corresponding royalty). In January 1798 he concluded further leases on the property, and one of these authorised him to construct his own tramroad to connect his coal and ironworks with a new shipping place on the mudflats at Llanelly. Raby's 'new iron way' was built on

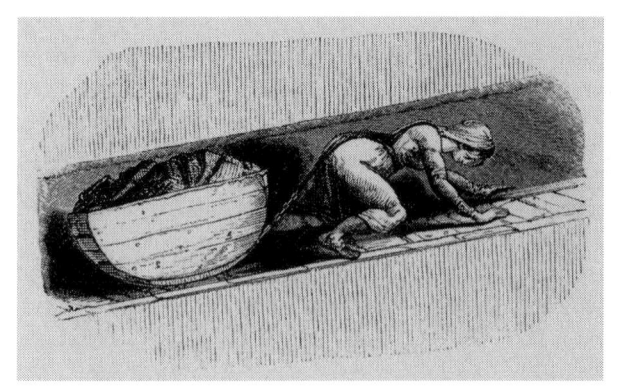

Children working in a coal mine - against the regulations

Roger Bowen

the alignment of an earlier waggonway which had linked the Caemain pit with what was then the beach at Sandy. Alexander Raby's dock was a short distance to the north-west of Pemberton's Dock, and it later became known as the Carmarthenshire Dock. This dock and the tramroad serving it came into use by 1799. The most notable feature of the tramroad was an iron bridge over the River Lliedi at Sandy, which is believed to have been the world's third iron railway bridge.

A canal was still under consideration to connect the collieries in the hills with the harbour at Llanelly, but it was realised that the hilly terrain was difficult for canals, and from 1800 Raby planned a tramroad instead. In 1801 he promoted the Carmarthen Railway or Tramroad; it obtained Parliamentary Authority on 3 June 1802 and was second only to the Surrey Iron Railway in doing so. Capital was £25,000 and it was to use the trackbed of a former waggonway. It was also used to construct a harbour at the mouth of the River Lliedi. The Act empowered the company to acquire Raby's dock and tramroad system, and provided for the extension of the line to Castell-y-Garreg, about 3½ miles west of Llandybie. The tramroad was a plateway, using L-shaped plates so that ordinary wagon wheels could run on it; the plates were supported on stone blocks. Although Raby had been the prime mover in consideration of tramways at Llanelly, the new Company was a joint-stock company, and there were several other shareholders. The engineer was James Barnes.

The gauge seems to have been four feet: the engineer's report of September 1801 stated his intention that the line should be built with 'rails laid 4 Feet asunder'. However Price records the recollection of an unnamed 'old retainer' on the estate: he wrote

"The Mynydd Mawr Railway was made 2 in. broder [broader] as far as Tyishaf Farm for convenience of coals from the Old Ship [the Old Slip, near Furnace]... The way we manage was Take off and put on washers on the axeltry [axletree] to width of 2 inches."

Price speculates that several earlier tramroads in the area were built to the gauge of 4ft 2in, but that the Carmarthenshire Railway (Tramroad) was built to match the gauge of Raby's line, rather than the

Victorian Physician

others.

The first section of line was opened for traffic from the ironworks at Cwmddyche to the water's edge at Llanelly in May 1803, a distance of one and a half miles. This is claimed to be the first publicly authorised railway in use in Britain, because the Surrey Iron Railway, although authorised earlier, was not ready for traffic until July 1803. In fact by then the first five miles of the Carmarthenshire Railway (Tramroad), together with certain branches, were already in use. Earthworks were considerable for a tramroad, and the ruling gradient was limited to 1 in 38.

By November 1803 the line was open as far as Brindini (Cynheidre), at an altitude of 500 feet above sea level. A considerable embankment was necessary on Mynydd Mawr itself, which delayed opening there until November 1804 and the line was completed to Gorslas (Cross Hands) in 1805. During the construction process near Cross Hands several outcrops of anthracite coal were discovered.

The line flourished, and in November 1805 plans were considered

Pit pony at work in mine

Roger Bowen

for further improvements to the dock at Llanelly. There were numerous branch connections to industrial premises mostly under Raby's control, and the line was to be doubled 'from the turnout place at Lime Kiln [Cwmddyche] to the turnout place at Old Castle.' There was opposition to this from some of the London shareholders and it is not certain whether the doubling work was actually carried out.

There were financial difficulties in the company: at a shareholders' meeting on 7 November 1805 there was a clear body of opinion that Raby had diverted the company's resources to his own benefit. On 15 August 1806 a Special General Meeting was held, at which a report was presented outlining unauthorised branches built by Raby, and the fact that his own wagons had used the line without paying the toll. The financial criticism of Raby gathered pace and in June 1807 he was obliged to sell most of his industrial property to pay debts. Debt had been incurred on the railway too, and by November 1809 the commercial activity on the line was at a very low level. Raby continued his activities locally, although increasingly under the financial patronage of others, in effect a salaried manager. He left the area as a result of worsening finances in 1826.

Technical progress in railways had developed edge rails, which were capable of carrying heavier wheel loads, and it is likely that an edge railway had been built alongside the lower part of the Carmarthenshire alignment before 1832, by which time the now-outmoded Carmarthenshire Tramroad had fallen into disuse north of Felin Foel.

Carter records that the Carmarthenshire raised further subscriptions in 1834 for improvement works, and that the company was re-incorporated in 1864-5.

Thomas Kymer had made a 3.5 mile canal from his pits at Pwllyllygoed to a harbour at Kidwelly about 1769. In 1811 it was proposed to extend the canal to Pontyberem and also to Llanelly, and the Kidwelly and Llanelly Canal Company was formed to do so; in 1812 it obtained an authorising Act of Parliament, and the extensions were permitted to be canals or tramroads, to Cwm-y-Glo near Cwmmawr and to a basin at Llanelly. The canals were constructed and in operation, but neither the tramroad nor the connection to Llanelly were made until 1837, but the new facility at Kidwelly was an obvious competitive threat to the Llanelly interest.

Victorian Physician

It was the evident success of these enterprises that first attracted the attention of Charles Barron Norton who was a shareholder in some of the workings.

In 1835 the Llanelly Railway obtained powers to build from St David's Pit, above Dafen, to connect with the Carmarthenshire Railway at Felin Foel. The Llanelly Railway was to be an edge railway, and it seems to have been assumed that the Carmarthenshire line would be converted to that system; however this line was never built. From September 1839 anthracite coal from Mynydd Mawr was brought to Llanelly by the Llanelly Railway, by-passing the Carmarthenshire line, taking an easterly sweep through the present-day Ammanford).

The Great Western Railway supported a nominally independent South Wales Railway that was to connect Gloucester (and thence London over the GWR) with Fishguard, forming a route to Ireland by ferry and (it was hoped) in due course North America. This railway opened through Llanelly (from Swansea to Carmarthen) on 11 October 1852, although the western terminus was altered. The South Wales Railway was built on the broad gauge, for compatibility with the Great Western Railway. In 1858 the Llanelly Harbour Commissioners obtained Parliamentary authority to build a broad gauge branch line from the SWR to the western harbour breakwater, closely following the Carmarthenshire alignment.

The South Wales Railway had been conceived as a partner with the Great Western Railway, but the financial aspect of the relationship was somewhat shaky. However, in 1862 the Great Western Railway absorbed the South Wales Railway. The broad gauge was increasingly a liability in South Wales, where much of the activity of extracting coal took place in areas served by local, narrow gauge lines, and the transshipment to broad gauge wagons was a massive deterrent. The Great Western Railway determined to convert the gauge of its lines in South Wales to what had become "standard" gauge, d did so in May 1872.

Roger Bowen

8
THE NORTON FAMILY TRUST

*I am a little collier and gweithio underground
The raff will never torri when I go up and down
It's bara when I'm hungry
And cwrw when I'm dry
It's gwely when I'm tired
And nefoedd when I die.*

The English translation is the following:

I am a little collier and working underground
The rope will never break when I go up and down

*It's bread when I'm hungry
And beer when I'm dry
It's bed when I'm tired
And heaven when I die.*

Women did not work underground at Gwauncaegurwen although the law prohibiting them did not come before the Mines Regulation Act of 1842, but women worked on the surface at Mountain Colliery,

Victorian Physician

Cwmgors. The employment of boys under ten years of age was forbidden by the same Act. After 1842, the day's work was supposed to be twelve hours a day, but often the colliers, accompanied by boys, prepared the " arms" and notched the "collars" of the timber on top of the incline until 10.0 p.m. For this extra work the men paid for cakes for the boys in a Braint, which was a special kind of wedding reception known as Taithin in Carmarthenshire, and Neithior at Alltwen and Clydach. This was an important function, held when a pair got married. Here they sold beer, mead, tea and cakes, but they paid only for the cakes to avoid tax and licence. The ceremony lasted a week or a fortnight, and sometimes a month or two. The proceeds, which often amounting to £20 to £40, went to the married couple which gave them a good start to their married life.

With the passing of the 1864 Act, the number of working hours underground was reduced from twelve to ten, but this Act was often broken, especially in Levels and Drifts where underground workmen seldom saw sunlight, except on Sundays. Eight hours a day was the aim at the end of the nineteenth century, as shown in the Jingle-

Wyth awr o weithio;
Wyth awr yn rhydd;
Wyth awr o gysgu
A wyth swllt y dydd.

(Eight hours work; Eight hours play; Eight hours sleep; And eight bob a day.)

At the pits in 1850 miners won the coal from narrow single stalls, and conveyed the coal in home-made wicker carts, fixed on skids. Coal carted down to levels was filled into home-made trams with flat wheels without a projection on the side of the rails, which consisted of iron plates on wood. The manager prohibited the colliers from filling more than 15 cwts. on a tram, otherwise the rails would be bent and broken. Very little timber was used to support the roof, so pillars about four yards wide were left between the stalls, which might be six yards wide with a good roof, or three yards wide with a bad roof.

Roger Bowen

Collieries were on a small scale, and wages based on a system of individual bargaining. Employers and workmen had little corporate organization, and minor local disputes often occurred. Some idea of the conditions facing the Norton concern as they restarted the colliery in Cross Hands will be the days of the *Sliding Scale of 1875*, when wages fluctuated, with sometimes a rise and other times a fall. Before 1848, a rise from 2 1/2 per cent to 10 per cent was granted, but in 1840 and 1850 there were falls of 10 per cent. Two years later, wages were lowered by 5 per cent. Another slump took place in 1868, when the anthracite collieries worked only three days a week. During the Franco-Prussian War in 1871-1872 demand for anthracite increased and 10 per cent. was added to the wages.

However, after the coming of the *Sliding Scale in 1875*, even when the price of coal was at its lowest, the collieries worked more regularly, and thus benefited the community. *The Sliding Scale in the Anthracite District* really began in 1862. Five collieries in the Pontardawe district signed the agreement, namely Gwauncaegurwen, Brynmorgan, Cawdor, (a Norton pit) Collieries of Amman Iron Works, and Mountain Colliery (Gwaith y Focsen), Cwmgors. The other collieries who did not sign also followed the *Sliding Scale*. *Miners Combined* before the Sliding Scale; and the Anthracite collieries were divided into three districts, and Enoch Rees, Brynamman, acted as secretary. They advocated improvements in safety, ventilation, lighting and reduction of working hours in mines, as well as the removal of the *Truck System*, which was the paying of wages of workmen in goods from the company shop instead of money.

Female labour underground was prohibited by the 1842 Act, and in the same Act the employment of boys under ten years of age was prohibited. Evidently this part of the Act was not enforced, as many boys under ten years continued to work underground at Brynamman, Gwauncaegurwen, Cwmgors, Cwmllynfell and Ystalyfera until 1856.

In 1860, checkweighers were allowed, and in the 1887 Act, miners' pay depended on the amount of coal won by them. The amount of coal was ascertained by placing a weighing machine near the pit mouth. Checkweighers, paid for by the miners, checked the weights,

Victorian Physician

Henry Norton, son of Charles Barron Norton and brother of Dr John Howard Norton

Roger Bowen

The old brewary where the carmarthen interests of the Nortons started

but they were not allowed to interfere with the working of the mine. In the 1864 Act, the number of hours underground was reduced from twelve hours to ten hours a day. This Act was not vigorously enforced.

Owners looked askance at the formation of unions or any interference with management. On the back of the pay sheet of P. Budd's works at Ystalyfera was printed:

"Rule 9-Any workman combining with others to stop the Works, or attempting to interfere with the management of any department, or threatening to do so, in order to obtain dismissal of any person employed therein, or in order to compel any such person to join any union or society; and any workman who shall threaten or molest any

Victorian Physician

Charles Henry Norton (pictured in 1899)

Roger Bowen

person employed in the Works for the purpose of compelling such person to join such union or society shall be dismissed, without notice."

Norton & Co were large owners of collieries in the period from 1855 to 1882, their colleries being Cross Hands (the oldest), Mynydd Mawr, Cawdor and California and the most profitable product was anthracite. The large lump of anthracite that can be viewed to this day in the front garden of Swansea Museum, came from the Cross Hands mine as a present from the Nortons to Swansea City.

Dr John Howard Norton drew his final breath on 1st August 1874 at his home, Nant Glas, near Llanon. His had been an eventlful life which had its disappointments and difficulties.

He was married in 1840 to Elizabeth Tucker and between them they had 8 children of whom 6 survived into adult life. The first born was Elizabeth Norton (1842 -1865) in Mwldan in Cardiganshire.

Henry Norton (1818-1893) was brother to Dr John Howard Norton, the son of Charles Barron Norton. He was mayor of Carmarthen and a JP. He was born in Longstone Hall Bakewell in the county of Derbyshire. He married Margaret Evans in 1851 and between them they had 10 children. Henry worked as a Brewer alongside his father and also was a partner in the firm of Norton & Co, coal mine operators.

His children were Elizabeth, born 1846 who died in London in 1917. In 1849 Henry was born in 1849 in Langwad and became a brewer just like his father and grandfather before him. The extraction of coal came later.

Victorian Physician

Henry Norton JP, Mayor of Carmarthen

Roger Bowen

9
MINING IN DIFFICULT TIMES

And you as well must die, belovèd dust,
And all your beauty stand you in no stead;
This flawless, vital hand, this perfect head,
This body of flame and steel, before the gust
Of Death, or under his autumnal frost,
Shall be as any leaf, be no less dead
Than the first leaf that fell, this wonder fled,
Altered, estranged, disintegrated, lost.
                    Edna St. Vincent Millay

At least as early as the 6th century, the Druidic legendary person Ceridwen is associated with cauldrons and intoxicating preparations of grain in herbs in many poems of Taliesin, particularly the Hane-Taliesin. This preparation, Gwîn a Bragawd, is said to have brought "science, inspiration and immortality".
The Welsh Triads attribute the introduction of brewing grains barley and wheat to Coll, and name Llonion in Pembrokeshire as the source of the best barley, while Maes Gwenith in Gwent produces superior wheat and bees.
The Anglo-Saxon Chronicle for 852 records a distinction between

Victorian Physician

"fine ale" and Welsh ale, also called bragawd. or braggot, is somewhat between mead and what we today think of as ale. Saxon-period Welsh ale was a heady, strong beverage, made with spices such as cinnamon, ginger and clove as well as herbs and honey. Bragawd was often prepared in monasteries, with Tintern Abbey and the Friary of Carmarthen producing the beverage until Henry VIII dissolved the monasteries in 1536.

In the Laws of Hywel Dda, meanwhile, a distinction is drawn between bragawd and cwrwf, with bragawd being worth twice as much. Bragawd in this context is a fermented drink based on cwrwf to which honey, sweet wort, and ginger have been added.

Welsh beer is noted as a distinct style as late as 1854, with a recipe made solely from pale malt and hops described in a recipe book of the time.

Wales, along with the rest of Britain, came under the influence of the temperance movement, along with a burgeoning Welsh moral code based on Presbyterian and other Non-conformist beliefs in relation to alcohol. This rested against a background of places where there has historically been a lot of heavy industry such as coal mining in south Wales and the north east. This has given some people the impression that all Welsh beers have been very weak. However, as with beers all over Britain, alcohol percentages vary.

At least as early as the 6th century, the Druidic legendary person Ceridwen is associated with cauldrons and intoxicating preparations of grain in herbs in many poems of Taliesin, particularly the Hanes Taliesin. This preparation, Gwîn a Bragawd, is said to have brought "science, inspiration and immortality".

The Welsh Triads attribute the introduction of brewing grains barley and wheat to Coll, and name Llonion in Pembrokeshire as the source of the best barley, while Maes Gwenith in Gwent produces superior wheat and bees.

The Anglo-Saxon Chronicle for 852 records a distinction between "fine ale" and Welsh ale, known as bragawd. Carmarthen United Breweries Ltd, John Street, Carmarthen, Dyfed was registered 1890 to acquire Norton Brothers (founded by 1847), Springside; David Evan Lewis & Sons, Merlin Brewery and Evans & Son,

Roger Bowen

all of Carmarthen.
Acquired by Buckley's Brewery Ltd. in 1900 and brewing ceased.
THenry Norton senior was elected as the Town Mayor for Carmarthen in 1859 and 1871. The family's business interests were in coal deliveries in several parts of Carmarthenshire and in the South Wales Valleys. They also had a brewery in Carmarthen during the late 1890's but information on this is very hard to come by.
Several of the brothers* played rugby for Carmarthen Wanderers with Derwent Norton being one of only three players from 1875 to the present to have captained the team for a total of five seasons. He has the distinction of being the first ever team captain of Carmarthen Wanderers (1875-1910) / Carmarthen Harlequins (1911-1946) and Carmarthen RFC (1947-2017).
One match report shows William Barron Norton as having played for the Wanderers in the 1877/78 season when he would have been 15 years old. His other brother Talbot also turned out regularly during the club's early years.
Frances Annie Margaret Norton married Frank Marshall in the 4qtr of 1887, their marriage was registered in Carmarthen in Wales. Her birth was registered in Carmarthen also in the 4qtr of 1852.
    Frances lived in 1861 with her parents and four siblings, at Green Hill, Carmarthen, Carmarthenshire. Henry was a 'Common Brewer & Coal Proprietor', aged 42 born in Longstone Hall, Derbyshire. He is most probably the Henry Norton found on the IGI, bap 27 Sep 1818 at Great Longstone, Derbyshire, parents Charles & Elizabeth Norton.
William Norton born on the 28th April, 1862, was the fifth son of the late Mr. Henry Norton, J.P., of Green Hill, Caermarthen. He served an apprenticeship to Mr. J. A. B. Williams, who was at that time Borough and Water Engineer of Cardiff. He wasubsequently employed by Mr. Williams on surveys and drawingsin connection with the new water-supply to that town, and in 1886 and 1887 acted as Resident Engineer on the Llanishen Reservoir and Filter-beds, which formed part of the works. He also filled a similar position on the relieving storage reservoir at Blackbrook. From 1888 to 1895 he was em-

Victorian Physician

ployed under Mr. Harpur, Borough Engineer of Cardiff, on surveys and drawings for new roads and bridges, and an ornamental park lake of 32 acres, the construction of which he afterwardssuperintended. In 1895 Norton went to Manchester, where he was engaged under the City Surveyor, Mr. de Courcy Meade, for three years. In August, 1898, he was appointed one of the Engineers to the Niger State Protectorate. There he unfortunately contracted pneumonia, which proved fatal on the 11th December, 1898. Mr. Norton was elected an Associate Member on the Gth December, 1892.

James Lees Norton was born in 1865 at Carmarthen, Carmarthenshire, Wales. He was the son of Henry Norton and Margaret Evans who married Blanche Gwendoline Blandy, daughter of Adam Fettiplace Blandy and Elizabeth Mary Stradling-Carne, in 1868 at Abingdon, Oxfordshire.

The children of James Lees Norton and Blanche Gwendoline Blandy were Josephine Elizabeth Margaret Norton born 1904 and Mary Gwenlliam Blandy Norton in 1906.Adam Henry Williams Petre Norton1 b. 7 Sep 1909, d. 1994

Roger Bowen

10
JOHN HOWARD NORTON DIES

Pity me not because the light of day
At close of day no longer walks the sky;
Pity me not for beauties passed away
From field and thicket as the year goes by.
Edna St. Vincent Millay

John Howard Norton lived an interesting and varied life. From his birth in rural Derbyshire in 1815 until his somewhat early death in 1874 his career encompassed the medical profession as a general physician followed by a while in general practice. He studied the treatment of the insane and and opened an asylum with varied success. He trained for entry to the medical profession at a time when young men of his social standing would have found it very difficult to gain entry into a recognised medical school. Probably it was the encouragement of his father who was himself an army surgeon that infuenced his chosen career.
He was helped on his way by the apprenticeship he was awarded with a Sheffield apothecary. Then, after s spell in Italy he worked as a general practiioner in Southampton for some years.
Upon returning to his father's family in South Wales he became heavily involved in the mining of coal in parternship with his faather and brothers.

Victorian Physician

John Howard Norton's obiturary appeared soon after his death in *The Welshman* and is reproduced here:.

THE LATE JOHN HOWARD NORTON, ESQ., M.D. Dr. Norton died at his residence, Nantglns, Cross Hands, near Llannon, on the 1st instant. His illness- which his relatives date from about October last- he himself and they attributed simply to dyspepsia. Being a member of the Medical Club, Spring Gardens, London, lie had every opportunity—of which lie availed himself —of consulting his medical brethren, amongst whom are some of the most eminent men in the profession; but they failed to detect the precise nature of his complaint. On the 22nd July he left London for Nantglas for a change of air, but no perceptible improvement was observable. On the 27th ult. he wrote a long note (four pages) in a cheerful strain to his brother, stating I am writing on my back in Dod, afraid to move and disturb a fearful sciatica inflicted on me in addition to my other little troubles." These are his own words. On the 30th ult. he was up for several hours, went into his study and transacted some business, into his dining-room and talked pretty cheerfully with his family, he walked round the grounds and garden for some short time, and then retired to bed. His brother accompanied by an old intimate and mutual friend, visited him on the 31 st ult., and were astonished and grieved to see so marked a change in his health. He barely recognised either of them. We may state, on the authority of his nearest relatives, that the unre- mitting and even affectionate attention of Dr. Lewis, of Thornhill, to Dr. Norton (his patient) is deserving of the deepest gratitude on the part of his family and relatives. On the 31st ult. Dr. Lewis suggested that some eminent physician should be called in to consult with him on the case. A telegram was at once sent to Dr. Padley, of Swansea, who arrived the same evening. He, however, in common with Dr. Lewis, considered the case hopeless. On Thursday evening Dr. Norton told his medical attendant that he knew he was dying, and without a murmur of complaint gave up his life to the God who gave it. From this time he became almost unconscious, and at 11.15 p.m. on the 1st instant, he died without a

Roger Bowen

groan or gesture, and as his nurse says, as if he were going to sleep, and with a placid smile on his face." Dr. Norton was born in May, 1815, at Eyan, in Derbyshire, on the High Peak, and was the eldest son of Mr. Charles Barron Norton, of this town. Having received what in his youth was considered to be a liberal education, he was articled in his 18th year to a surgeon at Sheffield. Being of a most studious turn of mind, he devoted every leisure moment to reading and study, with the view of qualifying himself for the practice of medi- cine. He enjoyed the acquaintance of an eminent physician in Sheffield, who strongly advised him to take a course of studies in the medical schools and hospitals of Paris. To this end he devoted himself assiduously to the acquirement of the French language, and in the course of a little more than a year (having great aptitude for the learning of languages) he could read and speak French fluently. About the year 1837 he entered his name at the Ecole do Medicine in Paris, and attended the lectures of the day on medicine, surgery, chemistry, and the physical sciences. On the completion of his course at Paris he entered at the University of Edin- burgh, and took the degree of M.D. Subsequently he went to London and received his diploma as M.R.C.S., &c., and in 1842 or 1843, having received an appoint- ment under the Neapolitan Government, he went to Palermo as Medical Superintendent in that city. Returning in about two years, he practised at South- ampton for eight or nine years, Having made mental disease a special study, he established a Sanatarium and Lunatic Asylum at Amroth Castle, in Pembrokeshire, where he remained about ten years. Being of a versatile disposition, he joined his brother, Mr. Henry Norton, of this town, in the arduous operation of re-opening the Cross Hands collieries, which had been then closed for some: years. Dr Norton was a Churchman of the Broad School, but was tolerant of every religious section of the Christian Church and contributed to their Chapels and schools, with as much pleasure as to his own. In political warfare he was not equally urbane, being an advanced Liberal he was impatient of half-moaures, but his rancour ceased when the fray was over, and he would at once fraternise with his fiercest political foe.

Victorian Physician

Roger Bowen

11

THE EXTENDED NORTON FAMILY

From the ashes a fire shall be woken,
A light from the shadows shall spring;
Renewed shall be blade that was broken,
The crownless again shall be king."
.R.R. Tolkien, The Fellowship of the Ring

Dr John Howard Norton had two brothers and a sister all of whom moved with father, Charles Barron Norton, to South Wales in around 1840.
They were a very successful family group who maintained good contacts for the duration of Charles life (that ended in 1860) and after the death of John Howard in 1874. The eldest of the brothers was John Howard who was born in 1815. He was followed by William in 1816 and Henry in 1818 and finally by Jemima in 1820. The first three were born in Derbyshire and Jemima in Cheadle, Cheshire.
William Norton was born in Alport, Derbyshire and died in 1873 in Laugharne, South Wales. He worked in close harmony with his father who established both the brewery and a pub in Llanelli in 1841. The brewing interest then became the *Carmarthen Brewery*

Victorian Physician

that was reistered as owned by Norton & Sons in around 1850. As mentioned elsewhere the brewing interests were sold following amalamation with the well-known modern brewery interest of Buckley Ltd.

William Norton married M A R Warren in 1846. William then made a second marriage in 1846 to Mary Evans.

The next brother was Henry Norton JP (born 1818) who was also a brewer in partnership with his other brothers. Henry became Mayor of Carmarthen from 1859-1873. One of his chalidren is recorded at home:

Frances, daughter of Henry at home in 1861 with her parents and four siblings, living at Green Hill, Carmarthen, Carmarthenshire. Henry was a 'Common Brewer & Coal Proprietor', aged 42 born in Longstone Hall, Derbyshire.

The last born child of Charles Norton was Jemima born in 1820. She married John Gould Avery in 1847 and died in Hampstead in 1883.

John Howard Norton had seven children starting with Elizabthe Norton born in Mwldan in 1842. She married Wilfred Higginson in 1865. the next to be born in 1845 was Charles Henry in Millrook, Southampton. He married Elizabeth in 1867.

Then came Mary Norton born in Stoneham, Shirley, Southamton 1846 who married Thomas Wade in 1873. She died in Penzance in 1890.

Howard John Norton was born in 1848 and died in Brixton in 1904. He married Marion Jane Burman in Bungay in 1871. Esther Norton was born in 1849 in Southhampton.

Then followed Juliana Norton who was born in 1851 in Amroth Castle. She married Dr Henry Davis Male in 1876 in East Chinnock, Somerset.

Anne Robibnson did not surve for many months in 1853. Finally William Talbot Norton was born in Amroth Castle in 1858 and married Mary Jane Hawkins in 1898 in London.

Upon the death of William Norton an obituary appeared in *The Welshman*:

the many friends of William Barron Norton, who resided for some

Roger Bowen

twelve years in Cardiff, will regret to hear of his death, from pneumonia, in Old Calabar (West Africa) on the 17th ult. The deceased gentleman was the fifth son of ten children – seven sons and three daughters – of the late Alderman Henry Norton J.P. of Greenhill, Carmarthen and was about 37 years of age. Intelligence of his death reached his brothers at Carmarthen this week through the deceased's London agents, Sir Benjamin Macgregor, Bart & Co.
Mr Norton left Queen Elizabeth Grammar School Carmarthen for Shewbrooks' educational institution, Cardiff, being subsequently articled to civil engineer to Mr. Williams of the Cardiff Waterworks, and afterwards served for several years under the Cardiff Corporation.
Leaving to take up the post of civil engineer to the Manchester Corporation, he stayed in that city for a length of time. He was, whilst there, advised by some friends, to apply for an appointment in the Public Works Department in Africa with the Foreign Office. His communication with the Foreign Office was successful and in August last he was sent out to the West Coast of Africa to Old Calabar to take up an important remunerative post vacant in the Public Works Department. A month ago he wrote home quite cheerfully; the next communication was a wire announcing his death.

The most famous of the Norton progeny was undoubtedly William Norton (William Barron Norton (1862 – 1898) who was a Welsh international rugby union three-quarter who played club rugby for Cardiff Rugby Football Club and international rugby for Wales. He was awarded six caps for Wales.

Norton was one of the earliest Welsh internationals and first represented his country in 1882, in the team's first ever encounter with Ireland. Captained by Charles Lewis, Norton entered a team containing ten new caps, after the Welsh team were humiliated in their inaugural game against England. Wales won the game making it the very first international victory for the team. Norton was re-elected for the next five matches, completing the entirety of the 1883 and 1884 Home Nations Championships. Wales lost both games of the 1883 Championship, and the opening two games of

Victorian Physician

the 1884 tournament, but were successful for the final game of the series against Ireland. The 1884 Irish game saw the Ireland team arrive two players short and were forced to borrow two Welsh players to complete their team. Although the last game of Norton's international career, he ended by scoring his only try for his country.

William played in International matches for Wales against England 1882, 1884, Ireland 1882, 1884 and Scotland 1883, 1884.

The extended Norton family worked in harmony throughout the nineteenth century and this was in no small part due to the direction of Charles Barron Norton who helped create the Norton Brothers partnership and then to his sons who carried the enterprises on. Dr John Howard Norton has a very successful start in life but experienced disappointment in his later medical career.

END

Roger Bowen

REFERENCES and NOTES

Preface

Beer in Wales - Wikipedia
Carmarthen United Breweries Ltd I The National Archives
Kellow Chesney, The Victorian underworld (Harmondsworth: Penguin, 1972)
Henry Mayhew in the Morning Chronicle, A visit to the cholera districts of Bermondsey, 24 September 1849 Henry Mayhew, London labour and the London poor (Introduction) (London: Penguin, 1985 (originally published 1851))
The Times, 20 November 1850
Pamela Horn, The Victorian town child (Stroud: Sutton, 1997)
Gertrude Himmelfarb, The idea of poverty: England in the eary industrial age, pp 376 - 377 (London: Faber, 1984)
Hymns ancient and modern, 1904 (hymn 573), (London: William Clowes & Sons, 1904)
The third verse of the hymn All things bright and beautiful, first published in 1848 in Hymns for little children, by CFH (Cecil Frances Humphreys), (London: Joseph Masters, 1848).

Chapter 1

Victorian Physician

William Norton was born in Prestwich, Manchester. He was a Turnpike Keeper and excisemanHe married Rachel Hodges on Boxing Day 1739 in Haslington Lancashire. ANTWICH is the name of an ancient Marliet-town, a Parish, a Poor Law Union, a Rural Deanery, and a Hundred in the south of Cheshire

The Parish includes the Townships of Nantwich, Alvaston, Woolstanwood, and part of Willaston. Leighton, formerly included in Nantwich Parish, became in 1840 a new ecclesiastical districft, under the name of Leighton- cum-Minshull-Vernon, in the parish of Middlewich. Situated about the centre of the Hundred, old writers locate Nantwich on the "Great and Direcft Road from London to Holyhead," one hundred and sixty-nine miles from "Hick's Hall,"* and twenty miles from Chester. Since the introduftion of iron roads,

the situation of Nantwich must be referred to the modern and rival town of Crewe ; from which railway centre it is about four miles distant on the Crewe and Shrewsbury branch of the London and North Western Railway System. Rachel was born in 1711.

As a turnpike keeper William attended a road block on a major road in Prestwich and collected tolls. The Nortons had six children:

The first of these, born in 1730. was Michael Norton who died in 1707. The second, Holden Norton, was born in 1733 and died in 1804. Robert Norton was next but died in infancy as did his sister Martha. William Norton was born in 1740 in Stretford and died in 1773 in Manchester. He was a calico printer. Finally Thomas Norton was born in 1748and died in 1793 in Prestwich.

William Norton's son was Henry Norton born in Manchester in 1766 who died in 1828 in Matlock. His wife was Juliana Robinson (1787 - 1745) and they were married in 1787.

So we come ro Henry and Juliana's son, Charles Barron Norton, born in Manchester in 1787. He was the father of John Howard Norton who was born in 1815.

Carmarthen quotations from

Burnby, J.G.L. (1983) A Study of the English Apothecary from 1660 to 1760, Medical History, Supplement No. 3, 1983, The Wellcome Institute for the History of Medicine, London

Roger Bowen

Porter, R. (1997) The Greatest Benefit to Mankind: A Medical History of Humanity from Aniquity to the Present, Harper Collins

London Lives 1690–1800 Crime, Poverty and Social Policy in the Metropolis

Chapter 5

Reports of the Commisioners in Lunacy 1844, p.92 2. National Library of Wales, SD Ch/ Misc.25 ;Reports of the Commissioners in Lunacy (Supplemental) 1844, p.57; Powys Record Office, B/D/.ACA/2/ 292- 302 and National Library of Wales, SD/1827/87. The Reverend Richard Davies (c I777-1859), matriculated at Christ College, Oxford, in 1794, BA 1798, MA 1800, Archdeacon of Brecon 1804, Canon, St David's 1805. Vicar of Brecon until his death. Joseph Phillimore matriculated at Christ Church, Oxford, in 1793, BA 1797, BCL 1800, DCL 1804, Regius Professor of Civil Law 1809-1855 from Alumni Oxoniensis (1715-1885) p.350 and p.l 106 3 The Cambrian, (9 August 1889.) Joint Archive Service for Mid and South Glamorgan CO/94/7; and Pembrokeshire Record Office PQ/AL/1/21 Reports of the Commisioners in Lunacy (1844) p.210; and The House of Commons Journal, Vol 22, 1822, p.51, pp.1 19-120 and p.367. Reports of the Commisioners in Lunacy (1844), pp. 45-67, p. 134 and p. 186 and 1863 p. 98; British Sessional Papers Vol XVIII, (1824) p. 180; 1841

Chapter 6

"South Wales (geological map)". Geological Maps of Selected British Regions. Southampton University website. Retrieved John Fisher biography at First World War.com
Churchill, Sir Winston Biography at The encyclopedia of Earth Davies, John; Nigel Jenkins; Menna Baines; Peredur I. Lynch (2008). The Welsh Academy Encyclopaedia of Wales. Cardiff: University of Wales Press. ISBN 978-0-7083-1953-6.
Jenkins, Philip (1992). A History of Modern Wales 1536-1990. Har-

Victorian Physician

low: Longman. p. 366. ISBN 0-582-48925-3.
"Jobs to go as South West Wales coal mine is mothballed". South Wales Evening Post. 2015-06-26. Retrieved 2016-08-20.
Graham Day (1 January 2010). Making Sense of Wales: A Sociological Perspective. University of Wales Press. pp. 29–. ISBN 978-0-7083-2310-6.
Bloor, M. (2002). "No Longer Dying for a Living: Collective Responses to Injury Risks in South Wales Mining Communities, 1900-8". Sociology. 36 (1): 89–105. doi:10.1177/0038038502036001005. ISSN 8 "Welsh Mining Disasters". Welsh Coal Mines. Retrieved 15 April 2016.
"Offenders uncover 1860 Risca mine tragedy stone plaque". BBC. 27 September 2010. Retrieved 15 April 2016.
Geoff Coyle (22 April 2010). The Riches Beneath our Feet: How Mining Shaped Britain. OUP Oxford. pp. 97–. ISBN 978-0-19-161397-5.
"Senghenydd: Centenary of UK's worst pit disaster marked". BBC. 14 October 2013. Retrieved 15 April 2016.
"Aberfan disaster: Poignant service marks 48 years since the tragedy that killed 144". Walesonline. 22 October 2014. Retrieved 15 April 2016.
"Trapped Miners: Two Men Found Dead In Wales". Sky News. 16 September 2011. Retrieved 16 September 2011.
John Graham Jones (15 November 2014). The History of Wales. University of Wales Press. pp. 122–. ISBN 978-1-78316-169-0.
Robert Woods (5 October 2000). The Demography of Victorian England and Wales. Cambridge University Press. pp. 246–. ISBN 978-0-521-78254-8.
Arthur McIvor; Ronald Johnston (2007). Miners' Lung: A History of Dust Disease in British Coal Mining. Ashgate Publishing, Ltd. pp. 57–. ISBN 978-0-7546-3673-1.
Friedlander, D (1973). "Demographic Patterns and Socioeconomic Characteristics of the Coal-Mining Population in England and Wales in the Nineteenth Century". Economic Development and Cultural Change. 22 (1): 39–51.

Roger Bowen

The many friends of William Barron Norton, who resided for some twelve years in Cardiff, will regret to hear of his death, from pneumonia, in Old Calabar (West Africa) on the 17th ult. The deceased gentleman was the fifth son of ten children – seven sons and three daughters – of the late Alderman Henry Norton J.P. of Greenhill, Carmarthen and was about 37 years of age. Intelligence of his death reached his brothers at Carmarthen this week through the deceased's London agents, Sir Benjamin Macgregor, Bart & Co. Mr Norton left Queen Elizabeth Grammar School Carmarthen for Shewbrooks' educational institution, Cardiff, being subsequently articled to civil engineer to Mr. Williams of the Cardiff Waterworks, and afterwards served for several years under the Cardiff Corporation.

Leaving to take up the post of civil engineer to the Manchester Corporation, he stayed in that city for a length of time. He was, whilst there, advised by some friends, to apply for an appointment in the Public Works Department in Africa with the Foreign Office. His communication with the Foreign Office was successful and in August last he was sent out to the West Coast of Africa to Old Calabar to take up an important remunerative post vacant in the Public Works Department. A month ago he wrote home quite cheerfully; the next communication was a wire announcing his death. Great Sympathy.

ancestry.com; familysearch.org; FreeBMD; Sussex PhotoHistory

NOTICE is hereby given, that the Partnership heretofore carried on by John Howard Norton, William Norton, and Henry Norton, as Brewers, at the Carmarthen

Brewery, in the town of Carmarthen, has been dissolved by mutual consent; and .in future the business of-the .Carmarthen Brewery will be carried on by the said Henry Norton on his own separate account.—Dated this 29th day of July 1852. John Howard Norton. William Norton. Henry Norton.

Brewing in Llanelly in 1820 - 1870

Norton Bros and Carmarthen Breweries Llanelli become Buckleys in 1870.

Acknowledgement

I would like to thank Julie Jones, (nee Julie Norton) for the use of her extensively researched archive of family trees and other associated information.

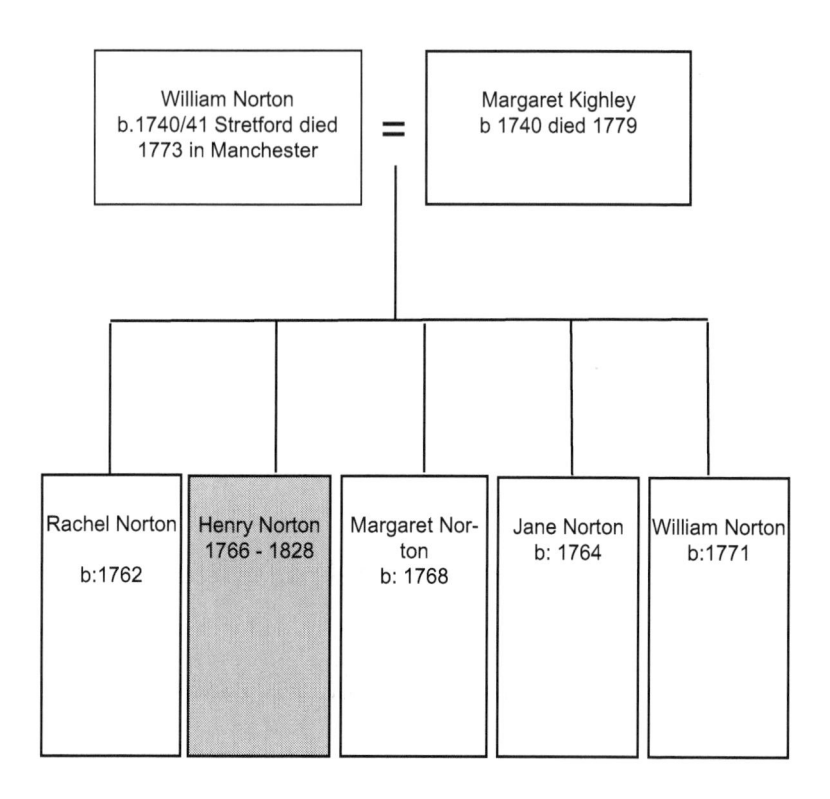

```
┌─────────────────────────┐     ┌─────────────────────────┐
│   William Norton        │  =  │   Margaret Kighley      │
│ b.1740/41 Stretford died│     │   b 1740 died 1779      │
│    1773 in Manchester   │     │                         │
└─────────────────────────┘     └─────────────────────────┘
```

| Rachel Norton b:1762 | **Henry Norton 1766 - 1828** | Margaret Norton b: 1768 | Jane Norton b: 1764 | William Norton b:1771 |

The first of the Nortons on record

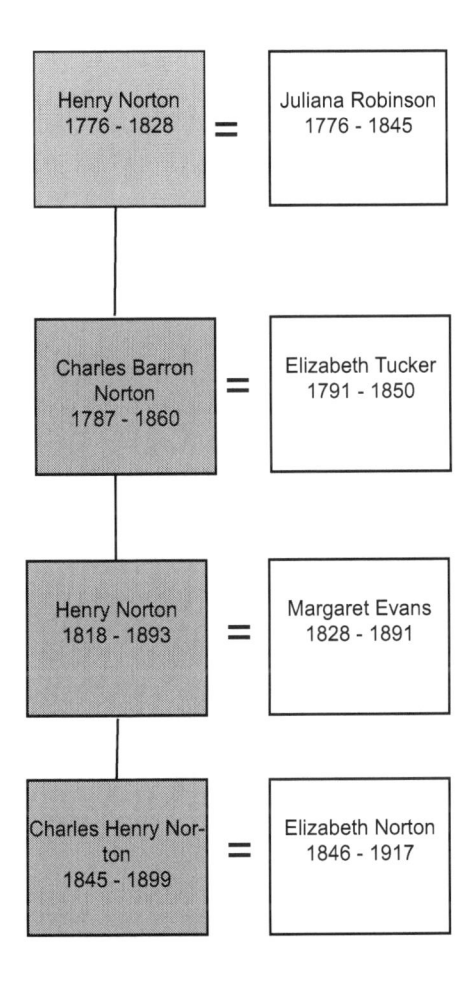

```
Henry Norton      =   Juliana Robinson
1776 - 1828           1776 - 1845
      |
Charles Barron    =   Elizabeth Tucker
   Norton              1791 - 1850
 1787 - 1860
      |
Henry Norton      =   Margaret Evans
 1818 - 1893          1828 - 1891
      |
Charles Henry Nor-=   Elizabeth Norton
    ton               1846 - 1917
 1845 - 1899
```

The Nortons up to the start of the nineteenth century beginning with Henry Norton, son of Charles Barron Norton, brother to Dr John Howard Norton

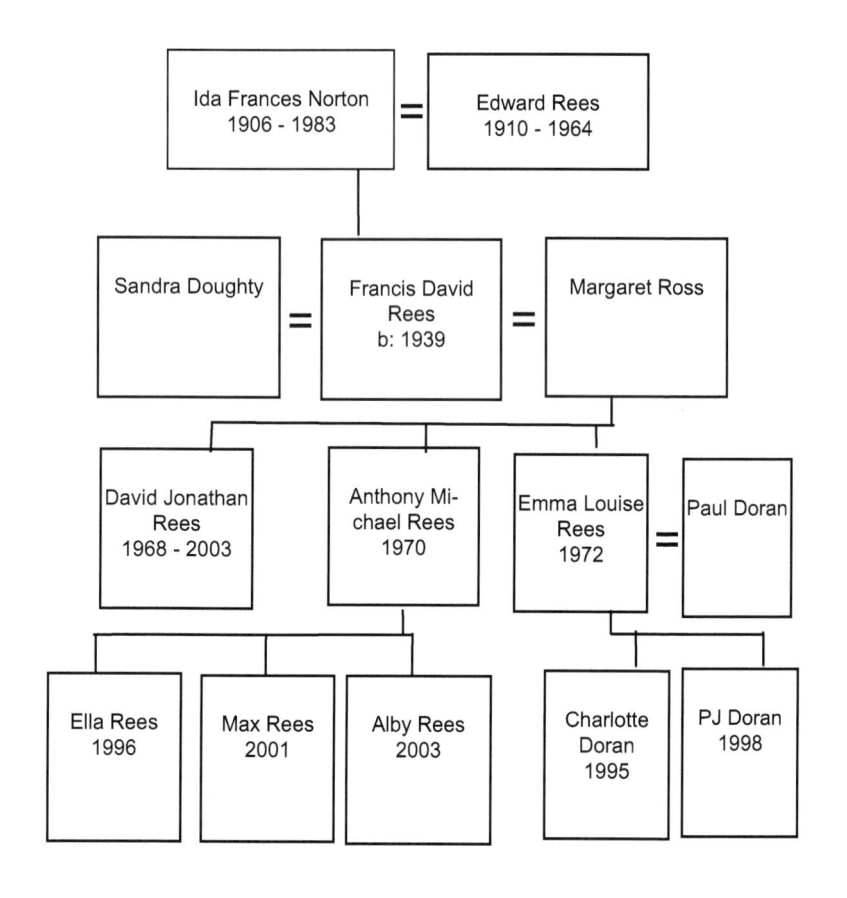

```
                    Ida Frances Norton  ═  Edward Rees
                       1906 - 1983           1910 - 1964
                              │
          ┌───────────────────┼───────────────────┐
   Sandra Doughty  ═   Francis David Rees   ═   Margaret Ross
                            b: 1939
                              │
          ┌───────────────────┼──────────┬─────────────────┐
   David Jonathan      Anthony Mi-      Emma Louise   ═   Paul Doran
        Rees           chael Rees          Rees
     1968 - 2003          1970             1972
                              │                 │
                   ┌──────────┼────────┐        ├──────────┐
              Ella Rees   Max Rees  Alby Rees  Charlotte  PJ Doran
                1996       2001      2003       Doran      1998
                                                 1995
```

The children and grandchildren of Frank Bayley Norton

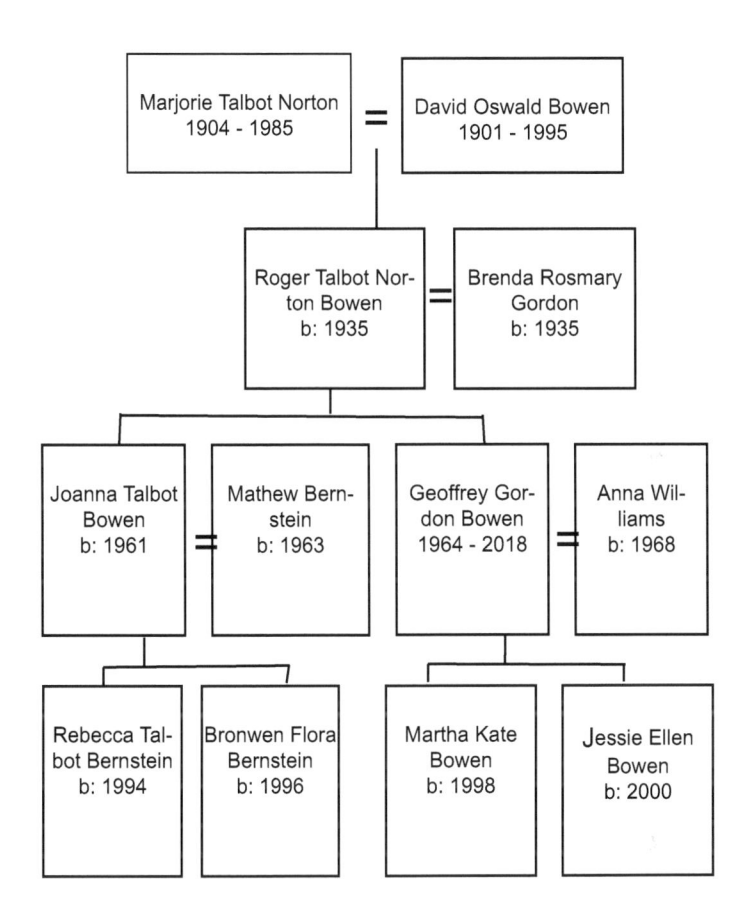

```
┌─────────────────────┐     ┌─────────────────────┐
│ Marjorie Talbot Norton │ ═ │ David Oswald Bowen  │
│    1904 - 1985      │     │    1901 - 1995      │
└─────────────────────┘     └─────────────────────┘
                    │
        ┌─────────────────────┐     ┌─────────────────────┐
        │ Roger Talbot Nor-   │ ═ │  Brenda Rosmary     │
        │    ton Bowen        │     │      Gordon         │
        │     b: 1935         │     │     b: 1935         │
        └─────────────────────┘     └─────────────────────┘
                    │
┌──────────┬──────────┬──────────┬──────────┐
│ Joanna   │ Mathew   │ Geoffrey │  Anna    │
│ Talbot   │ Bern-    │ Gor-     │ Wil-     │
│ Bowen    │ stein  ═ │ don Bowen│ liams  ═ │
│ b: 1961  │ b: 1963  │ 1964-2018│ b: 1968  │
└──────────┴──────────┴──────────┴──────────┘
        │                        │
┌──────────┬──────────┐  ┌──────────┬──────────┐
│ Rebecca  │ Bronwen  │  │ Martha   │ Jessie   │
│ Talbot   │ Flora    │  │ Kate     │ Ellen    │
│ Bernstein│ Bernstein│  │ Bowen    │ Bowen    │
│ b: 1994  │ b: 1996  │  │ b: 1998  │ b: 2000  │
└──────────┴──────────┘  └──────────┴──────────┘
```

The children and grandchildren of Frank Bayley Norton

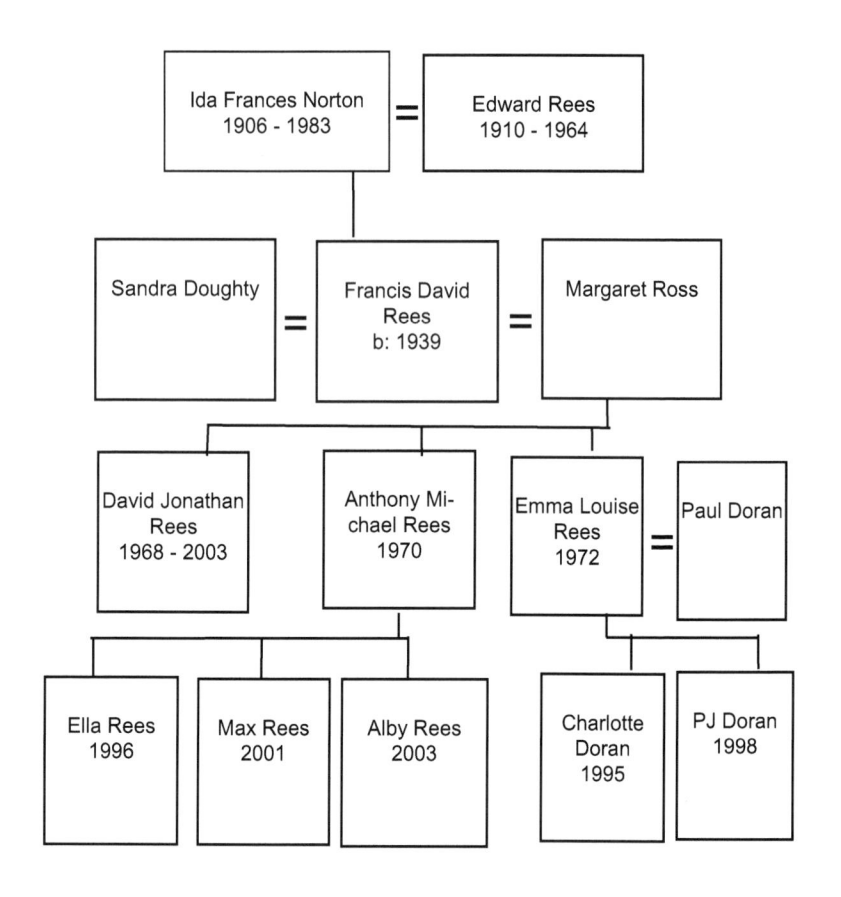

```
                    Ida Frances Norton  =  Edward Rees
                       1906 - 1983         1910 - 1964
                              |
          ┌───────────────────┼───────────────────┐
   Sandra Doughty  =  Francis David Rees  =  Margaret Ross
                          b: 1939
                              |
     ┌────────────────────────┼────────────────────────┐
  David Jonathan        Anthony Michael        Emma Louise Rees  =  Paul Doran
      Rees                   Rees                    1972
   1968 - 2003               1970
                              |                        |
              ┌───────────────┼──────────┐        ┌────┴────┐
         Ella Rees       Max Rees    Alby Rees  Charlotte   PJ Doran
           1996            2001        2003      Doran        1998
                                                 1995
```

The children and grandchildren of Frank Bayley Norton

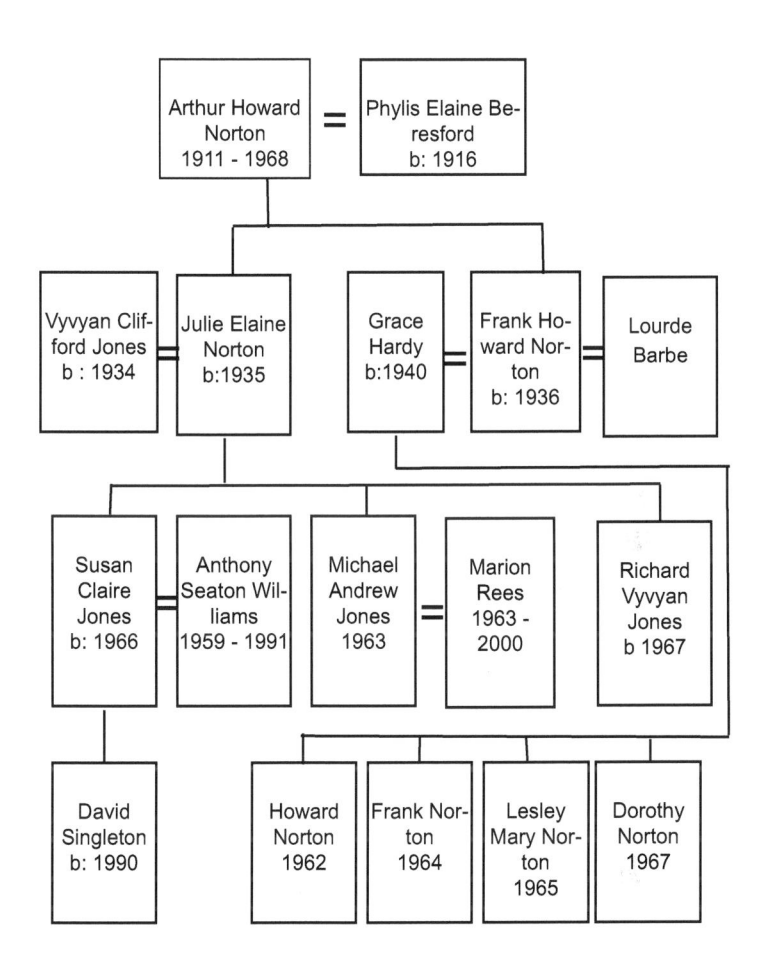

```
┌─────────────────────┐     ┌─────────────────────┐
│  Arthur Howard      │  =  │  Phylis Elaine Be-  │
│     Norton          │     │     resford         │
│   1911 - 1968       │     │     b: 1916         │
└─────────────────────┘     └─────────────────────┘
```

| Vyvyan Clifford Jones b : 1934 | = | Julie Elaine Norton b:1935 | Grace Hardy b:1940 | = | Frank Howard Norton b: 1936 | = | Lourde Barbe |

| Susan Claire Jones b: 1966 | Anthony Seaton Williams 1959 - 1991 | Michael Andrew Jones 1963 | = | Marion Rees 1963 - 2000 | Richard Vyvyan Jones b 1967 |

| David Singleton b: 1990 | Howard Norton 1962 | Frank Norton 1964 | Lesley Mary Norton 1965 | Dorothy Norton 1967 |

The children and grandchildren of
Frank Bayley Norton

Victorian Physician

LUNACY TO CROQUET
Roger Bowen

This is the story of the life of Thomas Nadauld Brushfield who became one of the first psychiatrists in Britain. He trained at the famous (or infamous) Bedlam hospital in London's East End and was appointed to be the chief medical officer of a newly established and pioneering lunatic asylum.

After he was gravely injured following an attack by one of his patients he retired to Budleigh Salterton where he became a leading figure at the famous croquet club.

As president of the Devon Literary Society he is remembered as a pioneering figure in the literary interests of the late nineteenth century.

AMAZON

THE CURATE AND THE GENERAL
Roger Bowen

Colonel Stringer Lawrence met Robert Palk when they both joined the army in India.
Lawrence was an army officer of the old school who brooked no interference with his military method though he struck up an immediate friendship with the Reverend Robert Palk.

Sir Robert Palk became a gifted administrator and it is due to his negotiating skills combined with promoted General Lawrence's military success that the East India Company survived French competition to become the major trading partner of Britain in India.

AMAZON

Other books by Roger Bowen include:

Anthology of Children's poetry
'We think you ought to go'
Swansea Exile
General Goodwyn
Memoirs
Do You Remember

Available from Amazon

Printed in Poland
by Amazon Fulfillment
Poland Sp. z o.o., Wrocław